Instant Healing

Think often of one or two famous sayings.

Out of every ten things in this world eight or nine will not go as I wish; and there is a mere handful of people I can communicate with.

Supposing we accept this, there will still be at least two things out of every ten that do go as we wish. I can't help you too much, all I can do is to tell you to think of those 'one or two' things, to turn your mind to happy things, to magnify the light of happiness, to keep the sadness in your heart at bay.

Susan Shumsky, DD

Instant Healing

Gain Inner Strength,
Empower Yourself,
and
Create Your Destiny

This edition first published in 2013 by New Page Books, an imprint of
Red Wheel/Weiser, LLC
With offices at:
65 Parker Street, Suite 7
Newburyport, MA 01950
www.redwheelweiser.com
www.newpagebooks.com

ISBN: 978-1-60163-239-5
Library of Congress Cataloging-in-Publication Data
humsky, Susan G.
Instant healing : gain inner strength, empower yourself, and create your destiny / by Susan Shumsky.
p. cm.
Includes bibliographical references (p.) and index.
ISBN 978-1-60163-239-5 -- ISBN 978-1-60163-559-4
1. Spiritual healing. 2. Mental healing. 3. New Thought. I. Title.

BL65.M4S485 2013
203'.1--dc23

2012027735

Cover design by Lucia Rossman/DigiDog Design
Interior by Eileen Dow Munson

Printed in the United States of America
IBI
10 9 8 7 6 5 4 3 2 1

For all who recognize the illusion of this world
And who long for the truth beyond,
For all who suffer the agony of separation
And who long for the exultation of unity:

Come now and open
To the divine presence within.
Come to the center of your heart.
Come here and find comfort.

Here you soothe your soul.
Here you return home
And find the solace you seek.
Here is a treasure for all who seek
The crown jewel of peace.
Here you are made whole again.

Instant Healing can familiarize readers with the complex subject of spiritual healing, affirmation, and prayer, but in no way claims to fully teach the techniques described. Therefore, personal instruction is recommended.

Instant Healing is not an independent guide for self-healing. Susan Shumsky is not a medical doctor, psychiatrist, or psychologist, and she does not diagnose diseases or prescribe treatments. No medical claims or cures are implied in this book, even if specific "benefits," "healing," or "treatments" are mentioned. Readers are advised to practice the methods in this book only under guidance and supervision of a qualified medical doctor or psychiatrist, and to use these methods at their own risk.

Susan Shumsky, Divine Revelation®, Teaching of Intuitional Metaphysics, New Page Books, and any other affiliate, agent, assign, licensee, and authorized representatives make no claim or obligation and take no legal responsibility for the effectiveness, results, or benefits of reading this book or of using the suggested methods; deny all liability for any injuries or damages that readers may incur; and are to be held harmless against any claim, liability, loss or damage caused by or arising from following any suggestions made in this book or from contacting anyone listed in this book or at *www.divinerevelation.org*.

Contents

Part Three:
Making Dreams Come True

Foreword

All healing is instant at the moment we accept our wholeness, goodness, and divine perfection as a spirit soul. What takes time is our acceptance. Doubt, which must be overcome, is our greatest challenge. That is because the outer appearances of lack, disease, and problems can be so convincing as if they are absolute, when they are, in fact, simply the effect of prior causes. They can and will change when there is a different cause. Outer appearances or manifestations in the body, mind, and affairs are caused by our previous thoughts, beliefs, and actions, and are not the truth at all, but an effect.

Dr. Shumsky has expertly dealt with the issue of doubt, fear, and lack by writing and offering affirmative prayers and affirmations that give us a powerful way to convince ourselves of our divine perfection, healing, and divine, godlike abilities and powers.

Affirmations, like mantras, are statements of a higher truth than what we have previously recognized or accepted. Although, at the moment of acceptance, it seems obvious to us that we are prosperous, happy, healthy, and loved, the process of getting to the obvious and higher truth involves hearing and reading sacred knowledge of a higher reality than what we have accepted and believed previously. Repetition of affirmations and mantras is most important until we accept these concepts beyond a shadow of a doubt.

Just because there are beliefs and concepts held in common and accepted as truth, that does not make these concepts absolute, but merely concepts. It isn't common for people to know and accept they are eternal as well as divine, godlike beings possessing amazing powers, qualities, and abilities that defy the accepted norm for a human being.

Dr. Shumsky has meticulously and magnificently written powerful affirmations that give us the words and sacred knowledge that penetrate the wall of fear and lack that has held humanity encased in limitation causing all manner of unnecessary difficulties. These affirmations will set them free.

When we first start on this spiritual path, the truth may sound like a lie, for we have been programmed to believe that the false is true and what is true is false. Sometimes we will believe that it is impossible to be blissful, prosperous, and loved, and that an affirmation or mantra is not true, but misery and lack are. The degree to which we doubt our good is the degree to which we have been damaged by what we have been taught through the educational process of religion, culture, school, media, family, etc.

Only courageous people who are willing to rise above the disinformation and fear-based indoctrination from all these sources are able to claim their identity, awaken from the spell cast upon them, trust themselves, and claim their divine inheritance.

Dr. Shumsky, a friend to me and to all who receive her teachings in person and through her books, has again written a masterpiece of wisdom, guidance, and inspiration that is as holy water poured on a soul that now blossoms from the infusion of divine goodness, love, and joy.

Terry Cole-Whittaker, DD

Introduction

In a world of chaos and uncertainty, we are beginning to wake up to the reality that we can no longer depend on solid, steadfast institutions we previously counted on, even for our very survival. There is an increasing, sickening fear about the future, which is taxing our mental and physical health. As our lives and livelihood appear to be sliding into an abyss, there seems no way out of this madness.

How can we find a path to greater well-being? Is there a way to reverse the downward spiral of inner turmoil and frustration? This book provides an answer. It can help you find instantaneous transformation. By using simple prayer and affirmation formulas, you can experience immediate healing, comfort, and solace. You can discover self-empowerment and gain self-confidence. You can heal your body, mind, emotions, and environment. You can attain a state of inner strength and wellness as never known before.

This book is an open doorway for anyone to experience spiritual healing instantaneously. The methods offered here are not new. The nondenominational, universal techniques of spiritual healing used in this book have been proven millions of times by people who have used them during the last 150 years to change their lives within minutes.

In the Human Potential, New Consciousness, and New Age movements, and New Thought, Unity Church, Church of Religious Science, Science of Mind, Divine Science, Christian Science, and Centers for Spiritual Living, these field-proven powerful healing methods have been variously named Affirmation, Scientific Prayer, Affirmative Prayer, Spiritual Mind Science, Spiritual Mind Treatment, and Treatment. We are grateful to the amazing teachers who developed these methods. Some of them include:

- Phineas Parkhurst Quimby (1802–1866), "Father of New Thought," a miraculous, nationally renowned healer.
- Mary Baker Eddy (1821–1910), author *Science and Health with Key to the Scriptures,* founder of Christian Science.
- Emma Curtis Hopkins (1853–1925), author of *High Mysticism,* teacher of the New Thought teachers, including Ernest Holmes and the Fillmores.

- Malinda Cramer (1844–1906) and Nona L. Brooks (1861–1945), founders of Divine Science.
- Charles Fillmore (1854–1948) and Myrtle Fillmore (1845–1931), founders of the Unity Church.
- Ernest Holmes (1887–1960), author of *Science of Mind* and founder of the Church of Religious Science (not to be confused with Scientology, which is not taught in this book).
- Peter Victor Meyer (1912–2004) and Ann Meyer Makeever (1916–2007), coauthors of *Being a Christ*, founders of Teaching of the Inner Christ and Teaching of Intuitional Metaphysics.
- Louise Hay (b. 1926), author of *You Can Heal Your Life* and founder of Hay House.

Such New Thought teachers propose that all difficulties can be overcome through metaphysical remedies, such as prayer and affirmation. The method of Affirmative Prayer Treatment, also known as Scientific Prayer, is a process of "treating" (healing and transforming) your mind until it realizes the truth of God's eternal good behind the appearance of false limitations. Once your mind has been treated, it is ready to accept the action of the Spiritual Law (the Law of Perfection Everywhere Now) to demonstrate (materialize) your prayer.

Ernest Holmes, in *Science of the Mind*, defines this method of prayer as follows: "Treatment is the time, process and method necessary to the changing of our thought. Treatment is clearing the thought of negation, of doubt and fear, and causing it to perceive the ever-presence of God."

By transforming, healing, or "treating" your mind, you can change the outcome of actions previously set into motion by your former mind-set. By setting up conditions in your mind that allow God to work through the Spiritual Law, your transformation occurs. Then, you accept with full faith that the desired goal is achieved. In this way, the power of intention is used in order to achieve your heart's desires.

This book is the go-to handbook for anyone who wants to transform his or her state of mind or the surrounding mental atmosphere, in an instant. One of my previous books, *Miracle Prayer*, teaches a nine-step method to help you formulate Scientific Prayer Treatments. If you read that book, you learned how to compose the kinds of prayers you will find here. However, in this book, you are not required to learn anything in order to benefit from these amazing prayer techniques.

Here you will find 243 healing affirmation and prayer formulas. These methods are simple and effective, and require no background or training. All you need to do is read the formula out loud, and then let go and allow the magic to happen. The prayer methods in this book have already proven very potent and meaningful in the lives of millions of people. Through this book, you can now discover how the power of your spoken word, with intention, produces miraculous, instant results.

How to Use this Book

The prayers in this book are not associated with any particular religion. They are universal and can be applied to all religious paths and beliefs. You are welcome to change the words in the prayers to fit your own spiritual affinities. For example, if you want to call upon Goddess rather than God, please feel free to do so. If you prefer the name Hashem to the name Christ, please change it. If you desire to call upon Krishna, Buddha, or Allah, please go ahead and do that. Any other name of God/Goddess you favor is acceptable in these prayers.

All the prayers and affirmations in this book are listed in the Appendix on page 205. They are easy to find, listed by chapter, title, and page number. Simply go to the Appendix and look up what you want to pray for.

These prayers and affirmations are to be spoken audibly, in a strong, clear voice. Speaking the prayer audibly produces the greatest potency. If you are in a place or a situation where you cannot say the prayer out loud, then whisper it to yourself. You may repeat these prayers and affirmations as many times as you like. If you have a deep problem or want to manifest a desire, then say the prayer several times daily. Just keep repeating the prayer until you get the result you are seeking. Every prayer works. It either produces an instant result, or else it creates an instant healing that moves you toward your desired goal. So keep praying, and never, never, never give up.

When saying these prayers for family, friends, clients, pets, or others, simply replace the words *I* or *myself* with the name of the person or animal for whom you are praying. Make sure to get permission from others, or from their higher Self, before praying for them. Always respect other people's free-will choice, and do not trespass against anyone's will.

Every time you say one of the prayers in this book, please speak the prayer as if your higher Self is speaking through you. What does this mean? Your higher Self has unlimited power and authority. It is the mighty "I AM" presence, which is your inner divinity, God within you. In India, this presence is called *Atman.* If you speak with this kind of authority, your words will have potent manifesting power. Therefore, in your mind, just imagine your inner divine nature, your true Self, is speaking the prayer. When you say the mighty words "I AM," speak those words with a commanding, authoritative voice. Know your inner divinity is at work, manifesting the desired outcome.

Important Note: All the prayers and affirmations in this book can be used to heal yourself or can be reworded to heal others. Speak the prayers audibly with conviction, confidence, and certainty. To learn more about these prayers and how to use them, please read *Miracle Prayer* and *Exploring Auras.* To order a CD, downloadable files, or laminated cards of healing prayers, please visit *www.divinerevelation.org.*

Part One
Changing Your Mind

Gaining Inner Strength and Empowerment

I am the master of my fate: I am the captain of my soul.
—William Ernest Henley

The first step to self-mastery is self-authority, which means realizing you are the captain of your own ship of destiny. When you take mastery over your life, knowing you create your future through your thoughts, words, and deeds, no one and nothing can dissuade you from your divine plan and purpose. You walk the royal highway to glory.

Self-authority means you are in control. Yet, at the same time, you are led by a higher force that guides you. As you walk the straight path toward your goals, a brilliant light illumines the way. You are not seduced by crooked byways and detours leading you astray. You walk patiently, step by step, with full confidence and faith, knowing you are on the highest road.

Many people are weakened by the influences of others. They wander away from their divine purpose into dark, dank jungles of ignorance and delusion. Negative messages from parents, teachers, clergy, peers, the media, and other manipulative powers hold sway and weigh them down. Trapped in a web of confusion and fear, they have bought into prevailing attitudes shared by the collective human mind. Habits, conditions, patterns, and belief systems hold them in bondage. Many get lost in that jungle and never find their way out. But here, in this book, you can find the open doorway out of the shadows and into the light of wisdom.

Let us begin with the foundational affirmation of this book—an affirmation recommended as the staple in everyone's healing medicine cabinet.

1. Self-Authority Affirmation

The Self-Authority Affirmation is the most important, potent prayer in this book. It can transform your life instantaneously. With daily use, you can gain tremendous self-empowerment and confidence. This affirmation closes your energy field to lower levels of mind, and opens you to the spiritual world. Therefore, you are no longer subject to "environ-mental static"—negative vibrations and thought-forms around you.

With this affirmation, you can heal "Psychic Sponge Syndrome"—oversensitivity to the mental atmosphere. Psychic sponges absorb the vibrations around them as a sponge absorbs water. They tend to take on the ills of negative people in their proximity. Lower vibrations of heavy environments weaken them. Their life energy is sucked dry by psychic vampires all day. After a day's work in a dense, destructive atmosphere, psychic sponges feel drained and exhausted.

This affirmation can help you revive and restore your energy. Use it whenever you feel weak, afraid, powerless, off-kilter, or intimidated. It is recommended before you leave your home, before meditation, and before sleep. Use it whenever you need protection, self-empowerment, and confidence, such as when entering a crowded area, before meeting an authority figure, before and after meeting clients or business associates, and before tests, interviews, auditions, or meetings. When you feel drained by people or situations, or you feel an invasive or overshadowing energy, use this prayer, in or out of meditation.

I AM in control.
I AM one with God.
I AM the only authority in my life.
I AM divinely protected by the light of my being.
I close off my aura and body of light
To the lower astral levels of mind.
And I now open to the spiritual world.
Thank you, God, and SO IT IS.

2. Psychic Block Prayer

At times you may want to close off your aura to more than just the lower astral levels of mind. You may feel the need to close it off and provide protection against psychic attack or manipulation. In such cases, this prayer can help.

I AM in control.
I AM the only authority in my life.
I AM divinely protected by the light of my being.
I now close off my aura and body of light to
[Name of person, thing, or organization here]
And to all but my own God Self.
Thank you, God, and SO IT IS.

3. Prayer for Protection

The Prayer for Protection helps you maintain spiritual self-defense, divine protection, and intimacy with God. It allows you to feel God's presence and brings comfort, solace, and inspiration.

This prayer is used every Sunday in all New Thought churches, such as Unity Church and Centers for Spiritual Living. James Dillet Freeman composed this prayer in 1941, during World War II, to give comfort to soldiers in the trenches.

Use this prayer before entering meditation, receiving intuition, or doing healing work.

The light of God surrounds me.
The love of God enfolds me.
The power of God protects me.
The presence of God watches over me.
Wherever I AM, God is!
And all is well!

4. Divine Protection

You are never alone. God is always with you, providing divine protection. All you need to do is ask, by using this prayer.

I AM, right now and always,
In God's loving, protecting grace.
God's caring presence surrounds me
Today and every day, here and everywhere.
The angel of divine protection goes before me,
Preparing my way and guarding me
From any seeming negative experiences.
The power and presence of God
Shield me now and always.
Wherever I go, I AM in God's care and keeping.
I AM invisible, invincible, and invulnerable
To all seeming negative energies
And I AM now open to the light of God.
Thank you, God, and SO IT IS.

5. Safety and Protection for Travel

No matter where you go, you are safe and secure when you travel in the presence of God. The invincible armor of God surrounds and protects you anywhere and everywhere.

God is my perfect travel agent,
Who arranges my journey in divine order.
God is my perfect travel companion,
Who accompanies me on every pathway.

God's is my perfect timekeeper,
Who gets me to my destination in divine timing.
God is my perfect angel of protection,
Who stands above, below, and on every side of me.
God is my perfect bodyguard and safekeeper,
Who walks with me everywhere as my divine shield.
Thank you, God, and SO IT IS.

6. Divine Safety and Security

You are always safe in the arms of God's love. All that is needed is to affirm that security and protection in your life.

I AM always protected by divine love.
I trust the process of life.
My needs are always taken care of.
It is safe to be me. I now accept and approve of myself.
It is safe to feel. My feelings are normal and acceptable.
It is safe to experience joy. I now breathe freely and fully.
It is safe to change and grow. I now create my new future.
It is safe to see and experience new ideas and new ways.
I love life and life loves me. I AM open to life.
I AM receptive to all of God's good.
It is okay to feel good. It is okay to feel safe.
I deserve to feel good. I deserve to feel safe.
I now relax and let life flow joyously.
I AM safe in the arms of God's love.
All is well.
Thank you, God, and SO IT IS.

7. At Home in God

God sustains and supports all who call upon God in innocence with faith. All that is required is to ask with sincerity.

The breath of life is a gift from God,
Which nurtures, sustains, and supports me.
At home with God, I find rest and renewal every day.
Right where I AM, I AM at home in the presence of God.
Turning to the Spirit of God within,
I experience a true homecoming.
Thank you, God, and SO IT IS.

8. Pillar of Light Visualization

Visualization can help you create a powerful sphere of divine protection. Many people imagine a sphere, bubble, or column of light surrounding and protecting them. Here is a way to visualize divine protection, increase energy and charisma, and feel lighter and lifted.

Close your eyes and imagine a beauteous sphere of protective divine light of whatever color (white, gold, violet, pink, or another color) above your head. Then see a ray of that light streaming down through the midline of your body, all the way from the top of your head to the tips of your toes. Visualize this light ray vibrating and radiating from your energy centers, filling your entire energy field.

This beauteous light fills your energy field with divine love, invincibility, joy, and fulfillment. Feel this divine light vibrating and radiating within and around you. This light now expands beyond the boundaries of your energy field to create a pillar of divine light, which brings you strength, power, and energy. You are divinely protected by the light of your being.

9. Rod of Light

You can invoke spiritual awakening by visualizing God's light within you. The light rod of God is one of the ways God expresses through you.

A beauteous light rod of God is now established
In the very center and midline of my body.
This light rod extends from the top of my head
To the bottom of my feet,
Right down the center of my body.
This light rod of immeasurable beauty and glory
Blazes with pure God love and God light.
I AM centered, balanced, and protected
By that light rod of God, and I AM at peace.
Thank you, God, and SO IT IS.

10. Grounded in Spirit

There are many powerful ways to stay grounded, centered, balanced, and in control. Walking barefoot or imagining a cord reaching deep into the earth—this is not the way to stay grounded in Spirit. Being grounded means uniting with God, with your true nature of being. Use this affirmation to help you re-center in Spirit, whenever you feel off-kilter, out of your body, or out of touch with reality.

God's love fills and surrounds me with comfort.
God's light fills and surrounds me with peace.
God's energy fills and surrounds me with blessings.
I AM now lifted into God's holy presence,
Which fills and surrounds me with glory.
I AM a radiant being of light,
Living in the heart of God's love.
I AM bless-ed and belov-ed of God.
I AM now fully grounded in the presence of God.
I AM now centered, steady, and solid in God's love,
And I AM in profound peace.
Thank you, God, and SO IT IS.

11. Let There Be Light Prayer

Healing and lifting your energy field can fill your life with peace, joy, and light. Your subtle body can be transformed with two basic energies: light and sound. The following three prayers increase your light, and speaking these affirmations positively affects your field through sound. Use these to heal, cleanse, clear, awaken, lift to a higher vibrational octave, and connect with Spirit.

Let there be light. The loving, empowering,
White, golden, violet, pink, green, and blue
Healing, empowering, divine light
Of Babaji, the Holy Spirit, and [name of your deity]
In and through this divine, healing, empowerment
Cleansing and healing session and situation now,
For the highest good of ["myself" or name of person]
And all others concerned.
[Repeat all lines above at least three times.]
Thank you, God, and SO IT IS.

12. White Fire Affirmation

I AM now lovingly lifted, healed and cleansed
In the white fire of the Holy Spirit and Christ Consciousness,
And the violet consuming, purifying flame of Saint Germain,
Under God's grace, in God's own wise and perfect ways.
Thank you, God, and SO IT IS.

13. Golden Healing Prayer

I AM now lovingly filled, lifted, and surrounded
With the golden healing substance of God Consciousness.
I AM now filled with God's love, God's light, and God's truth.
God now fills my aura and body of light
With this golden healing substance,
Which closes the doors of both my physical and subtle bodies
To the lower astral levels of mind
And instead attunes me to God Consciousness.
This golden healing substance now heals and lifts me.
It awakens my awareness to God Consciousness within me
And within all of creation, now.
I AM now healed, and I AM more fully attuned
To God within me, and in all creation.
I lovingly awaken to greater awareness
Of God within me and around me, right now.
Thank you, God, and SO IT IS.

14. Energy Healing Prayer

Your energy field (aura) can be compromised in many ways. Psychic vampires can suck energy from it. Drugs, alcohol, cigarettes, or other addictive substances can damage it. Improper food, shallow breathing, negative thinking, or stress can diminish it. Playing with the occult without safeguards can invite lower energies that pierce holes in it. This prayer can repair, renew, and restore wholeness and oneness.

I call upon the Holy Spirit to lovingly restore my energy field
To its perfect, pristine state of wholeness and oneness.
My aura and body of light are now healed, lifted, and blessed
By the light of God's love and truth.
I AM now filled with the radiance of God
Which cleanses and heals my energy field.
God's medicinal, restorative light now mends
All seeming tears, rips, and holes,
And closes all portals, openings, and doorways
To lower astral planes and energies.
My aura and body of light are now whole and complete.
I AM free from any and all astral intrusion.

I AM now whole and at peace in the light of God's love.
Thank you, God, and SO IT IS.

15. Self-Integration Prayer

Some people feel parts of themselves have been lost or stolen, through neglect, influences of others, or even malevolent intentions of others. They feel something is missing, but cannot identify what. Such people move through life confused, scattered, fragmented, disintegrated, and disassembled. This affirmation can recall parts that appear to be missing, so wholeness can be restored.

I AM the resurrection and the life.
I AM perfection everywhere now.
My life is restored to wholeness.
My mind is restored to perfection.
My subtle body is complete and whole.
Any and all parts of myself that appeared to be
Shattered, fragmented, lost, stolen, or missing
Are now recalled and restored to my being.
They are recalled and restored to my being,
Recalled and restored to my being.
I AM now full, complete, and whole,
Filled with the light of God's love.
Thank you, God, and SO IT IS.

16. Inner Strength

This prayer can help you grow in spiritual strength, courage, and self-authority. When you rely upon God for your strength, then you are divinely protected and indomitable.

I now turn to God, wherein I find strength.
God is my comfort, my fortress, and my deliverer.
God is my rock, in which I take refuge.
I do not depend on things of the world
To give me courage and strength.
God's strength is established within me,
And I AM forever upheld.
I AM now made mentally, physically,
Emotionally, and spiritually strong in God,
And in the power of God's might.

I AM a tower of strength and stability.
The power of God is released in me,
And I AM daily changed into a likeness
More and more like God.
Thank you, God, and SO IT IS.

17. Divine Armor Prayer

When you are filled and surrounded with the radiance of God's love, nothing and no one can invade or intrude upon your energy field. A divine armor of invincibility protects you in all places and circumstances. Allowing God to be your divine protector is the best way to become invulnerable to lower energies.

I now open my heart to the bright sunlight of God's love.
The radiant light of God now pours into my being.
God's grace now fills and surrounds my energy field
With great beauty, great light, and great wholeness.
I AM now enclosed in a divine bubble
Of beauteous, iridescent, shimmering, radiant light.
This divine bubble is a golden, multicolored sphere
Of white, luminous purple, pink, blue, green, and silver light,
Filling, penetrating, and surrounding my energy field.
This beauteous, invincible sphere of light
Now heals, protects, and seals me.
I know all seeming holes, punctures, and piercings,
Which have torn my energy field, are now sealed
With the pure white cleansing fire of the Holy Spirit
And the beauteous golden light of God's love.
Thank you, God, and SO IT IS.

18. Treatment for Self-Authority

This book includes affirmations, prayers, and Prayer Treatments. Prayer Treatments can help you heal deep emotional blockages that prevent the positive transformation you are seeking. This Prayer Treatment can release whatever has been blocking your acceptance of self-authority and self-empowerment.

This is a treatment for myself, [*full name*], for perfect self-authority, inner strength, and self-empowerment, or better, now.

I recognize there is only one power and one presence in the universe: God the good, omnipotent. God is the ultimate authority and has supreme dominion. God is the director and manager of the entire cosmos. God, the invincible, is the one sovereign and the only power. God is wholeness and oneness. God is perfection everywhere now.

I AM now one with and merged with God in a perfect seamless wholeness. There is only oneness and unity between God and me. There is only one and one only. I AM unified with the authority and dominion of God. I AM my own sovereign and director now. I AM invincible wholeness and oneness. I AM perfection everywhere now.

I therefore claim for myself, [*full name*], perfect self-authority, inner strength, and self-empowerment, or better, now.

I now heal and release all limiting ideas and beliefs interfering with this claim, whether known or unknown, conscious or subconscious. My thoughts are now one with, the same as, and in tune with God's thought. I dissolve from my mind now any and all need to be controlled or dominated by anyone or anything. No person, place, thing, organization, situation, circumstance, memory, or addiction can possess me or hold me in bondage. I belong to God and to my Self alone. I AM free.

I dissolve any and all reluctance to take responsibility for my own decisions. I AM in dominion of my life now. I dispel all feelings of dependency on others. I AM independent and in command of my life. I let go of any seeming need to be a victim. I now know that no one and nothing can control me, and I AM in control of my own life now. I release any and all fear of expression, and I boldly express my Self exactly as I AM. I let go of feeling unworthy, undeserving, or unacceptable. I know now that I AM the expression of God, I AM the perfection of God, and I AM perfect for me for now. I AM worthy, deserving, and acceptable now.

I AM in control. I AM the only authority in my life. I AM divinely protected by the light of my being. I close off my aura and body of light to all but my own inner divinity.

I now fully accept, in consciousness, my perfect self-authority, or better, now. I thank God for manifesting this good in my life now, under grace, in perfect ways. Thank you, God, and SO IT IS.

Healing Emotions and Deep-Seated Beliefs

Change your thoughts and you change your world.
—Norman Vincent Peale

The very first verse of the first chapter of the Dhammapada, the foundation scripture of Buddhism, states, "All that we are is the result of what we have thought.... If a man speaks or acts with an evil thought, pain follows him, as the wheel follows the foot of the ox that draws the carriage.... If a man speaks or acts with a pure thought, happiness follows him, like a shadow that never leaves him."

In this verse, Buddha illustrates how you are the sole creator of your destiny through thoughts, words, and deeds. This is the fundamental precept of metaphysics. You are the author of your life. You write the script and act in your play. You are the producer, director, and stage manager. Nothing ever happens "to you." You only happen to yourself.

Lord Buddha's teaching can be summarized as follows: There are no victims; there are only volunteers. No one is to blame for your problems or is responsible for your successes, because you have created everything by what you think, say, and do.

In this vein, you can use healing affirmations and prayers to transform your mind from negativity to positivity. When you control your mind and speech, then you take the reins of your destiny. You can manifest your true heart's desires and create miracles.

19. Thought-Form Healing

The course of your life is determined by beliefs, habits, emotions, and intentions. For example, if you continually say, "I am fat, I am fat," then such strongly implanted thoughts take shape as thought-forms—deeply ingrained beliefs. Because your subconscious mind always says yes to every deeply felt and believed intention, the manifestation will occur, just as you pictured it.

Your mind is like a pond. When you drop a rock into the center, waves of water ripple outward in concentric circles until the ripples hit the outer edge. Then they ripple back to the center. Similarly, your thoughts broadcast from your mind out to the universe. Then they return to you, exactly as transmitted.

If your mind radiates positive, smooth, stable, joyful, peaceful, tranquil, content, serene, loving thoughts and feelings, then you magnetize positive experiences. However, if your mind is poisoned with negative, hateful, angry, vengeful, depressing, chaotic, anxious, irritating, jagged, toxic thoughts and emotions, then you attract difficult, negative situations.

This healing prayer is a way to take control of your thoughts with a simple formula. It can heal anything—any physical, mental, or emotional difficulty. The Thought-Form Healing is simple: feel, name, and release the negative thoughts; then replace them by naming and accepting positive ones.

The prayer has prompts that allow you to personalize it. At the first prompt, close your eyes and notice any negative feelings coming up for you. Name these thoughts and feelings and say them audibly. Then continue reading the prayer. At the second prompt, close your eyes and name positive feelings, the opposite correlates of the negative feelings named in the first blank space. Here are a few examples of negative thoughts and their positive correlates, which can help you to compose your prayer:

Negative Thoughts	Positive Correlates
Anger	Forgiveness
Sadness	Happiness
Guilt	Self-forgiveness
Blame	Self-responsibility
Depression	Joy
Hatred	Love
Self-hatred	Self-worth
Poverty	Abundance
Fear	Courage
Vengeance	Forgiveness
Insecurity	Confidence
Shyness	Outgoingness
Rejection	Self-acceptance
Doubt	Faith
Loss	Wholeness
Addiction	Self-authority
Illness	Wellness
Inflexibility	Flexibility
Egotism	Humility

Negative Thoughts	Positive Correlates
Condemnation	Commendation
Coercion	Permissiveness
Disrespect	Respect
Attachment	Letting go
Exhaustion	Vitality
Frustration	Nonresistance
Agitation	Serenity
Worry	Peacefulness
Evasion	Responsibility
Pressure	Resourcefulness
Burden	Letting go
Jealousy	Goodwill
Perfectionism	Self-love
Impatience	Patience
Error	Forgiveness
Selfishness	Altruism
Grief	Comfort
Confusion	Clarity
Aging	Youthfulness

With this powerful healing prayer, you no longer have an excuse to remain in a bad mood. You now have the power to change in a matter of moments.

I invoke the divine presence to eliminate
All negations and limitations that no longer serve me.
I now dispel all negations of [list negative thoughts here],
And any other thoughts and emotions
That do not reflect the truth of my being.
They are now lovingly lifted, transmuted, and transformed
Through the power of the Holy Spirit.
I AM now open and free to embrace
Positive, life-supporting, energizing thoughts and emotions.
I now welcome thoughts of [list positive correlates here].
I now let go of error thinking, and I accept the truth.
I AM in balance. I AM in control.
Thank you, God, and SO IT IS.

20. Thought-Form Healing: Short Form

The following is a shortcut version of the Thought-Form Healing. This brief prayer can be used just as effectively as the longer version you just learned.

I now heal and release all negations of
[List negative thoughts here]
And they are gone.
They are lifted into the light of God's love and truth.
I now welcome and accept thoughts of
[List positive correlates here].
Thank you, God, and SO IT IS.

21. Thought-Form, Pattern, and Belief-Structure Healing

Negative thoughts and feelings can become so overwhelming that they appear to take over your life. However, no habit, belief, or thought can control you when you use the power of prayer to heal it. As you read this healing prayer aloud, close your eyes when you come to the first prompt. Speak out whatever negative feelings and thoughts are coming up for you. At the second prompt, again close your eyes and speak the opposite correlates of the feelings that came up in the first prompt.

I call forth the Holy Spirit,
The spirit of wholeness, love, and truth,

To illuminate the truth upon any and all
Thought-forms, thought-patterns, and thought-structures
That obscure the truth in this situation now.
Through the healing light of the Holy Spirit,
I dissolve any and all negative thought-forms,
Structures, patterns, concepts, and belief systems.
The light of truth is completely permeating and suffusing
All negativity in this situation, place,
And states of consciousness related to it.
Any and all limiting thought-forms, thought-concepts,
Thought-patterns, and thought-structures
Are now easily and effortlessly dissolved
By the healing light of truth of the Holy Spirit,
And the law of first cause,
Into the nothingness of what they truly are.
Through the Holy Spirit power, they are now
Lifted, healed, and transmuted into the good,
And they are now gone.
[Take a deep breath to release.]
The Holy Spirit now shines upon, suffuses, lifts, and transmutes
Any and all negative thought-forms of
[List negative thoughts here]
Into their divine true archetypes of
[List positive correlates here].
They are now lifted, transmuted, and transformed
Through the power of the Holy Spirit, and the law of first cause.
I AM in control of my mind. I AM empowered now.
Through my inner divinity
And the divine light and lifting power of the Holy Spirit,
I AM divinely protected and guided into uplifted, true,
More powerfully God-conscious living and being,
Right here and right now.
Thank you, God, and SO IT IS.

22. Releasing False Beliefs

With God's help, you can let go of past negative beliefs, and embrace a powerful, positive future of ease, comfort, harmony, joy, and love.

I AM my divine indwelling thought-adjuster.
I have faith in God's life within me.

False beliefs and negative appearances
Have no power over me.
They are now dissolved
By the loving, forgiving action of God.
Centered in God's presence, I now let go
Of every negative thought, feeling, and concern.
I easily and comfortably release that which
I no longer need, and no longer serves my life.
God's perfect harmony is now expressed in my world.
I release all sense of hardship and struggle,
Remembering God is my gentle and loving guide
And all is well.
I release from my mind all that is unlike love and joy.
I let go of the past
And welcome the new, fresh, and vital now.
Letting go is easy.
It is easy to reprogram the computer of my mind.
All of life is change, and my life is ever new.
Through freedom of Spirit, I AM a new me.
Thank you, God, and SO IT IS.

23. Façade Body Healing

A façade body is a set of beliefs so deeply entrenched that it forms a mental armor, mask, belt, prison, cage, or façade around you. Such a façade shuts out love vibrations and prevents expression of your true Self.

Before using this prayer, decide which deeply held belief you want to heal. For example, you might be wearing a façade body of poverty, of unworthiness, superiority, inferiority, machismo, timidity, fatness, defensiveness, bullishness, anger, or another mask. Choose a façade body and call it by name to describe it—for example, "victim," "self-righteousness," or "self-hatred." Place that name into the prompts of the prayer.

I call upon Holy Spirit
To lovingly shine the light of truth and love
Upon any and all façade bodies of
[Name of façade body]
Within myself now.
These façade bodies of
[Name of façade body],

Which are surrounding me,
Are now lovingly cracked open, crumbled up,
Dissolved, healed, released, and let go,
By the Holy Spirit, into the light of God's love and truth.
I now call upon my higher Self, my inner divinity,
To fill this space and to fill my energy field
With my true divine pattern and soul expression.
Let God's will be done in this matter.
Thank you, God, and SO IT IS.

24. Past Experience Healing Prayer

Your subconscious mind carries a burden of experiences and memories from your past, from this life and previous lives. These are stored in your subconscious mental body, as a computer hard drive stores data. This prayer will help you release the past so your energy field can be free from weighty yokes of false responsibility, guilt, blame, and resentment.

All experiences, core, record, memory, and effects
Are transmuted and transformed into pure love and light
By the violet consuming flame of limitless transmutation.
I have a clean blank slate on which to write new experiences.
I AM transformed by the renewing of my mind, right now.
I close all doors, openings, and holes to my past now.
I AM vibrating at such a high frequency of love,
That I AM free from all past burdens and false responsibilities.
I AM a divine being of great love, light, and glory.
Thank you, God, and SO IT IS.

25. Letting Go Prayer

When you hold on to the past, your energy field is cluttered with dark, deep-seated, entrenched energies. Letting go of these vibrations lifts you to a higher, more refined frequency.

I let go of worn-out things, hopeless conditions,
Useless ideas, and futile relationships now.
Divine right order and divine right timing
Are now established and maintained
In my mind, body, relationships, finances,
In all of my affairs, and in my world,
Through the power of the Holy Spirit
And my indwelling God Consciousness now.

Divine circulation is at work in my life.
The inflow and outflow of everything in my life
Is established in divine order and harmony.
I AM peaceful, balanced, and poised.
Thank you, God, and SO IT IS.

26. Prayer Before Sleep

Use this prayer right before sleep to strengthen your energy field and prevent psychic attack or vampirism. This simple prayer can avert nightmares, fitful sleep, or broken sleep, as you sleep more soundly and peacefully.

I open my heart to God's love.
I AM filled with the light of God.
I AM a beloved child of God.
I AM a beauteous being of great power,
Great energy, great good, and great glory.
I call upon God to keep me protected, safe, and secure,
Within God's circle of protection, as I sleep.
I call upon God to build a beautiful golden sphere
Of divine love and light around me during sleep,
To keep me safe, secure, and one with God.
Thank you, God, and SO IT IS.

27. Treatment for a Positive Mental and Emotional Attitude

This is a treatment for myself, [*full name*], for a powerful, optimistic, and healthy mental and emotional mindset, and a positive, attitude and emotions, with accurate, truthful perceptions, or better, now.

I recognize there is only one power and one presence in the universe: God the good, omnipotent. God is the light of life, the truth of being. God is truth, and God sheds light and truth on all. God is the source of wisdom. God is good, very good perfection now. God is perfect mental and emotional health. God is the divine mental health provider. God is balance, equanimity, peace, and wholeness now.

I AM now one with and merged with God in a perfect, seamless wholeness. There is no separation between God and me. There is only oneness and unity. I AM the light of life, the truth of being. I AM filled with God's light, truth, and wisdom. God's good shines forth into my life in its fullness. I AM filled with the perfect mental and emotional health and well-being that God is. I AM one with the divine mental health provider that is God. I AM filled with balance, equanimity, peace, and wholeness now.

I therefore claim for myself, [*full name*], a powerful, optimistic, healthy mental and emotional mindset, and a positive attitude and emotions, with accurate, truthful perceptions, or better, now.

I now heal and release all limiting ideas and beliefs that interfere with this claim, whether known or unknown, conscious or subconscious. My thoughts are now one with, the same as, and attuned with God's thought. I dissolve from my mind now any and all need to cling to inaccurate, false beliefs. Whatever I think I have gained, in the past, from holding on to negative thoughts and emotions is now dissolved, released, healed, and let go from my mind, and it is gone. I release, loose, and let go of any and all seeming beliefs of pessimism, victimization, fear, anger, guilt, blame, sadness, unworthiness, limitation, frustration, anxiety, and depression. And they are gone. I no longer feel the need to adhere to false beliefs, habits, patterns, and conditions. I no longer feel seeming benefit from being a victim.

I now welcome, accept, and embrace new, positive, life-affirming thoughts and emotions of optimism, self-empowerment, courage, strength, love, forgiveness of self and others, self-acceptance, self-worth, self-love, limitlessness, contentment, peace, integrity, happiness, and joy. All false, limiting beliefs, concepts, and constructs that I have held are now dissolved, blessed, lifted, healed, released, and let go. I now welcome and accept accurate and truthful perceptions about myself. I AM now in charge of my life. I now take the reins of my life and I lead my own pathway in the direction of my highest good.

I now fully accept, in consciousness, my powerful, optimistic, healthy mental and emotional mindset, and positive attitude and emotions, with accurate, truthful perceptions, or better, now. I thank God for manifesting this good in my life now, under grace, in perfect ways, and I now release this prayer into the hands of God. Thank you, God, and SO IT IS.

28. Treatment for Healing Loss of a Loved One

This is a treatment for myself, [*full name*], for healing the loss of a loved one, or better, now.

I now know and recognize that there is one healing power and one healing presence at work in the universe and in my life: God the good, omnipotent. God is the light of my life, the truth of my being. God is the comforter. God is divine solace and consolation. God is the place of respite and relief. God is wholeness and oneness. God is love.

I AM now one with, merged with, and the same as God. In God I live, move, breathe, and have my being. God is within me and all around me. God is at the very center of my being—my very essence of being. I AM the comforter that God is. I AM the divine solace and consolation that God is. Within my Self is the place of respite and relief. I AM the wholeness and oneness that God is. I AM the love that God is.

I now therefore know and claim for myself, [*full name*], the perfect healing of the loss of a loved one, or better, now.

I now release from my mind any thoughts, feelings, and emotions that no longer serve me. My mind is now one with and the same as God's mind. I now release from my mind all thoughts of guilt, unfinished business, regret, self-reproach, remorse, separation, loneliness, isolation, sadness, grief, mourning, sorrow, anguish, and pain. These thoughts are now released, loosed, and let go now, and they are gone.

I AM now filled with new, beautiful, positive, powerful thoughts of self-forgiveness, letting go, letting God, overcoming, allowing, acceptance, peace, serenity, harmony, concord, love, wholeness, oneness, companionship, joy, freedom, truth, and fulfillment. I now accept divine comfort, solace, succor, relief, consolation, and respite. I dwell in the refuge and sanctuary of God, in the shelter of God's love. I now know and accept that there is no death, for the soul is indestructible. I know the love between my loved one and me is eternal and everlasting. I know my beautiful loved one lives on perpetually as an immortal soul, and therefore I do not grieve. I AM at peace.

I now fully accept, in consciousness, my perfect healing of the loss of a loved one, or better, now. I now let go and fully release this prayer into the Spiritual Law of Perfection Everywhere Now, knowing that it now manifests in my life, under God's grace, in perfect ways. Thank you, wonderful God, and SO IT IS.

Healing and Forgiving Relationships

Nobody can hurt me without my permission.
—Mahatma Gandhi

You are inextricably connected to the complex network of energy that covers this entire planet. Humans affect each other in profound ways, as we continually collide with each others' energy fields. Some effects, such as love and goodwill, are positive. Others, such as manipulation, control, exploitation, and coercion, are malevolent.

Your relationships can sometimes be loving, fulfilling, and harmonious, and at other times cold, distant, and discordant. However, you have the power to create the quality of relationships you want, through prayer. You can heal and transform your connections with family, friends, and coworkers. You can overcome psychic intrusions binding you to others in unhealthy ways.

29. Psychic-Tie Cut Healing

Psychic ties consist of undue attachments to or repulsions against any person, place, thing, organization, circumstance, memory, experience, or addiction that influence you adversely. They are built of negative thought-forms and emotions, and they are created without conscious intention. For example, if you have an argument with your boss, what is left over? A residue of energy, forming a psychic tie.

With clairvoyant sight, psychic ties appear as gray or black (or other color) ropes, cords, strings, webs, dreadlocks, or other nasty chain-like configurations attached to your energy centers. These shackles of energy are never helpful or beneficial. They serve no one. Therefore, all psychic bonds need to be severed and dissolved.

In contrast to psychic ties, love ties are true love bonds with your beloved ones, both alive and deceased. These ties also link you to God, your higher Self, angels, and spiritual inner teachers. These golden ties of true love can never be broken.

Because most people mistake psychic ties for love ties, they are reluctant to sever them. However, because psychic ties deplete energy and create physical disease, you realize how essential it is to cut them daily. In fact, I guarantee if you cut psychic ties with all coworkers in the office and all loved ones at home daily, you will have significantly better, more intimate relationships.

If you have a codependent or addictive relationship, then cutting psychic ties several times a day is crucial. Psychic ties are created every time you have sex, so it is vital to cut psychic ties after every sexual encounter. The umbilical cord attached to your navel from your mother still exists as a psychic tie in adulthood. It is essential to cut that tie, especially when your mother dies.

Use this prayer when you feel unduly attached to or repulsed by anything, when you are holding on to resentment, when you feel something or someone tugging on you, or to heal an obsession or addiction.

I call upon the Holy Spirit
To cut any and all psychic ties
Between myself and [name of person, place, thing, or addiction here].
These psychic ties are now lovingly
Cut, lifted, loved, healed, released, and let go
Into the light of God's love and truth.
I now welcome beautiful, divine, unconditional love ties
Filling the space between myself and
[Name of person, place, thing, or addiction here].
Thank you, God, and SO IT IS.

30. Psychic-Tie Cut Healing: Layer by Layer

This prayer will help you cut deep, seemingly impervious ties, heal an addiction or codependent relationships, and establish better, more loving relations.

I call upon the Holy Spirit to cut any and all
Astral and psychic ties and karmic bonds between
Myself and [name of person, place, thing, or addiction here].
These astral and psychic ties are now
Permanently and completely, lovingly, yet fully
Cut, cut, cut, cut, cut, cut, cut, cut, cut, cut, cut,
Cut, cut, cut, cut, cut, cut, cut, cut, cut, cut, cut,
Dissolved, dissolved, dissolved, dissolved, dissolved,
[Repeat the previous three lines until it feels complete.]
Lifted, loved, healed, blessed, forgiven,
Freed, loosed, released, and completely let go;
Layer by layer, layer by layer, group by group, group by group.
[Repeat the previous line until it feels complete.]
I now welcome beautiful divine unconditional love ties

Filling the space between myself and
[A person, place, thing, or addiction].
Thank you, God, and SO IT IS.

31. Psychic Bondage Healing

Use this prayer when a psychic tie has become bondage, and you have become a slave or imprisoned by it. This is helpful in cases of addiction or codependent relationships that have held you in chains.

I AM now released from psychic bondage.
All psychic ropes that have held me in chains
Are now lovingly untied and loosed, released, and let go.
All psychic nets that have imprisoned my energy field
Are now dissolved, blessed, lifted, and let go.
They are released into the nothingness
Of which they truly are.
I AM free from the bonds that have held me.
I AM in control.
I AM the only authority in my life.
I AM at peace.
Thank you, God, and SO IT IS.

32. Forgiveness Prayer

An unforgiving mental attitude is mired by psychic ties, nets, and chains binding you to past trauma, hate, and resentment. True forgiveness of self, of others, and of life situations dissolves binding ties and lifts your energy field quickly and profoundly.

Use the following forgiveness prayer daily to supercharge your spiritual growth and find happiness and fulfillment. Forgiveness is an ongoing, life-long project of highest importance.

By and through the power of the Holy Spirit,
I know and decree right now:
All that has seemingly offended me or held me,
I now forgive and release.
Within and without, I forgive and release.
Things past, things present, and all things future,
I now forgive and release.
I forgive and release everything and everyone, everywhere
Who can possibly need forgiveness or release.

This includes forgiveness for myself
Through the power of God now.
I forgive and release absolutely everyone and everything
Past, present, and future.
Everything and everyone from past, present, and future
That could possibly need to forgive and release me,
Including myself, does so now.
I AM free and all others concerned are also free.
Therefore all things are completely cleared up
Among us all, now and forevermore.
Thank you, God, and SO IT IS.

33. Forgiveness Healing Chant

This healing chant can forgive any particular person, group, or situation. You can work on a particular relationship, such as a parent, spouse, child, employer, or situation, for as long as you feel guided. With some relationships with lifelong difficulties, you might feel the need to use this for a year or more.

The God Consciousness in me
Is my forgiving and releasing power.
The God Consciousness in [name of person]
Is his/her forgiving and releasing power.
The God Consciousness in me
Is my forgiving and releasing power.
The God Consciousness in [name of person]
Is his/her forgiving and releasing power.
I AM free and he/she is free also.
Therefore, all things are cleared up between us,
Now and forevermore, under grace, in perfect ways.
Thank you, God, and SO IT IS.

34. Forgiveness Affirmation

In order to release and let go of people and situations in your life, forgiveness is essential. Use the prayer to clear up and move on from old seeming wrongdoings.

I now fully and freely forgive and release
[Insert name of person here].
I loose you and let you go.
You are free, and I AM free.
I let go and let God do perfect work in this situation

For the good of all concerned.
Thank you, God, and SO IT IS.
[Repeat until it feels complete.]

35. Divine Forgiveness

God forgives all seeming wrongs, so why is it so difficult to forgive ourselves? Imagine what it would be like to completely forgive yourself, with a life free from guilt and shame. Forgiveness of the relevant situation places it under the law of grace.

The forgiving, releasing, and healing power of God
Works in and through me now.
All judgment, resentment, criticism, and unforgiveness
Are now dissolved and healed.
With the love and peace of God within my heart,
I forgive everyone of everything—including myself.
I now forgive all past experiences.
I now forgive myself for all seeming
Errors, mistakes, and wrongdoings.
I bless myself. I AM forgiven. I AM free.
Thank you, God, and SO IT IS.

36. Healing Parental Patterning

This powerful prayer can help you deeply heal your relationship with the inner pattern represented by your parents, as they have demonstrated anything less than pure love. You can re-parent yourself by using this awesome prayer.

I now release any belief, perception, and judgment
That my father and mother did not hold me, hug me,
And love me every day until I was 5 years old.
I now release my belief, perception, and judgment
That my father and mother did not hold me, hug me,
And praise me every day until I was 10 years old.
I now release my belief, perception, and judgment
That my father and mother did not hold me, hug me,
And tell me how wonderful I was
Every day until I was 15 years old.
I now release my belief, perception, and judgment
That my father and mother did not hold me, hug me,
And tell me how much they accepted and approved of me

Every day until I was 20 years old.
I now release my belief, perception, and judgment
That my father and mother did not hold me, hug me,
Honor me, cherish me, and respect me every day of my life.
I now release my belief, perception, and judgment
That my father and mother are not with me any time I need
Them to hold me, hug me, love me, praise me, care for me,
Accept me, approve of me, honor me, cherish me, respect me,
And tell me how wonderful I AM.
I now hug, love, praise, care for, accept, approve,
Honor, cherish, respect, and value myself.
I now know and accept how wonderful I AM.
Thank you, God, and SO IT IS.

37. Canceling Contracts Prayer

An agreement, contract, or vow with a person, entity, or seeming dark forces can bind your energy field for lifetimes with psychic nets, clamps, traps, and jails. If you become aware of such energies affecting you or others, use the following affirmation to eliminate such bondage.

I call upon the Holy Spirit,
The Spirit of truth and wholeness,
To eliminate all binding contracts, vows, agreements,
Bonds, pacts, commitments, promises, and accords
That I have made at any time in any place
From this life and any previous lives,
Which no longer serve me.
All such binding contracts, vows, agreements,
Bonds, pacts, commitments, promises, and accords
Are now lovingly cancelled, loosed, healed,
Released, dissolved, and let go
Into the light of God's love and truth.
They are made null and void on every level
In every dimension, place, and time.
All thought-structures, matrices, frameworks,
Templates, molds, and patterns that were created
As a result of such agreements
Are now lovingly collapsed, dissolved, blessed,
Loved, healed, released, and completely let go.
They are lifted into the nothingness

Of which they truly are.
I AM free from all such vows and agreements now.
I AM in control. I AM the only authority in my life.
Thank you, God, and SO IT IS.

38. Perfect Loving Relations

By envisioning and affirming perfect, loving, harmonious relations with your loved ones, you can create that result. This prayer can help.

I AM united with God and with my loved ones
In a heartfelt spiritual connection.
Wherever we are, my loved ones and I
Are enfolded in the presence of God.
I see only God and good in my loved ones.
I AM free to be me, and I allow my loved ones
The freedom to be who they are.
I envelop my entire family in a circle of love—
Those who are living, and those who are dead.
I affirm wonderful, harmonious relationships with each one.
I see other people's viewpoints, and I AM blessed in doing so.
Thank you, God, and SO IT IS.

39. Treatment for Healing Relationships

This is a treatment for myself, [*full name*], for the perfect healing of my relationship with [*person*], or better, now.

I recognize God is unconditional love. God is the all-loving, all-forgiving healing presence and healing power that dwells within us and around us. God is perfect forgiveness and divine resolution. God is the resurrection and the life, the all-loving, all-merciful, and all-embracing. God is oneness and harmony. God is the consummate relationship counselor.

God is the only power at work in my life now. God's all-loving, all-forgiving divine presence restores me to oneness and harmony. God's divine mercy and unconditional love fill and surround me with peace. I AM the perfect healing presence and healing power now. I AM healed and resurrected by God's perfect forgiveness and divine resolution. I AM one with God's perfect counsel now.

I now therefore claim for myself, [*full name*], the perfect healing of my relationship with [*person*], or better, now.

I accept this perfect healing in my consciousness now. I now release all limiting concepts that interfere with this claim, whether known or unknown, conscious or subconscious. My thoughts are now one with, the same as, and in tune with God's thought. Perfect love dissolves all fear and anger in our relationship. Love now unites us in perfect harmony.

I forgive you now, dear [*person*], sending love from my heart, and I know you did the very best you could do in every situation with me; therefore, there is no guilt or blame. I now call upon the power of God to cut all psychic ties between myself and [*person*]. These psychic ties are now lovingly cut, lifted, loved, healed, dissolved, released, and let go by the power and presence of almighty God.

Dear [*person*], it is impossible for you to infringe upon my perfection. I recognize that you merely did what I invited, and, in reality, neither you nor anyone else can hurt me. I AM perfect now, always have been, and always will be, and you cannot change that. I pour out my heart in unconditional love toward you. The divine Self within me forgives you completely now. I visualize you before me in a beautiful sphere of golden divine light. Your inner beauty and radiance fill my being now with perfect forgiveness.

I now fully accept, in consciousness, the perfect healing of my relationship with [*person*], or better, now. I thank God for manifesting this healing in my life now. I release this claim to God and to the natural laws of creation. My claim demonstrates now by the power and the presence of God. That is the nature of natural law. AMEN.

40. Treatment for Healing Betrayal

This is a treatment for myself, [*full name*], for the perfect healing of any seeming betrayal in my relationship with [*person*], or better, now.

I now recognize God is perfect unconditional love and forgiveness. God is the all-merciful, all-loving, all-forgiving, all-compassionate presence and power in the universe. God is love. God is equanimity and equilibrium. God is wholeness and oneness.

God is here, there, and everywhere, within this, that, and everything. Therefore, God is within me and all around me. I AM now one with, merged with, and united with God in a perfect, seamless wholeness. In God I live, breathe, move, and have my being. God is my guide, my one light to cling to, my rock, my armor, my shield. God is here, within me, as perfect love and forgiveness. God as me is the all-merciful, all-loving, all-compassionate presence and power, the indwelling Spirit. I AM the love that God is. I AM the equanimity and equilibrium that God is.

I now therefore know and claim for myself, [*full name*], the perfect healing of any seeming betrayal in my relationship with [*person*], or better, now.

I now welcome and accept this perfect healing now. No matter what [*person*] has done, even if I considered it inexcusable, I know now that he/she always did the very best he/she could do. He/she acted in the best possible way he/she could, according to his/her level of consciousness at the time. I call upon the Holy Spirit to shine the light of forgiveness upon [*person*]. Even though I find it difficult to pardon or forgive his/her behavior, I now know the all-loving, all-merciful Father/Mother God forgives him/her completely.

I now let go of all need to betray or to be betrayed. I now release from my mind any and all thoughts of self-sabotage, self-hatred, self-betrayal, and self-punishment. I now let go of anger, resentment, frustration, disloyalty, treachery, unfaithfulness, and all other feelings that no longer serve me. These feelings are released from my mind, and they are gone. I AM now filled with pure, stainless, beauteous thoughts of peace, love, happiness, joy, forgiveness, letting go, allowing, acceptance, satisfaction, loyalty, constancy, trustworthiness, faithfulness, equilibrium, equanimity, oneness, and wholeness.

I now cut any and all psychic ties, karmic bonds, and binding connections between myself and [*person*]. These psychic ties are now lovingly cut, cut, cut, cut, cut, cut, cut, cut, cut, cut, cut, cut, cut, cut, cut, lifted, loved, blessed, dissolved, released, and completely let go into the light of God's love and truth.

I AM now free. I AM in control. I AM the only authority in my life. I AM divinely protected by the light of my being. I now close off my aura and body of light to [*person*], and to all but my own inner divinity.

I now fully accept, in consciousness, the perfect healing of any seeming betrayal in my relationship with [*person*], or better, now. I now release this prayer into the Spiritual Law, knowing it does demonstrate now, in my life, under grace, in God's own wise and perfect ways. Thank you, God, and SO BE IT.

41. Treatment for Perfect Harmonious Relationships at Home and Work

This is a treatment for myself, [*full name*], for perfect harmonious relationships in my life, or better, at home and work now.

I now know and recognize there is one power and one presence at work in the universe and in my life: God the good, omnipotent, omnipresent, and omniscient. God is perfect unconditional love. God's love is constant, dependable, unwavering, stable, immovable, eternal, ever-present, unreserved, and absolute. God is always present and never abandons anyone. God is ever and always faithful.

I AM now merged with, aligned with, united with, and one with God. In God I live, move, and have my being. I AM one with the power and presence of God, which is omnipotent, omnipresent, and omniscient. I AM one with God's perfect unconditional love. I AM the constant, dependable, unwavering, stable, immovable, eternal, ever-present, unreserved, and absolute love that God is. I AM ever-present and always faithful, as God is.

I now therefore know and claim perfect harmonious relationships in my life, or better, at home and work now.

I now know all my relationships are based upon perfect unconditional love. The love and relations I have with my parents, children, family, friends, colleagues, co-workers, teachers, students, employers, employees, and all other beings in my life are now perfect in every way, according to God's perfect will and guidance, for the very best for all concerned.

I now let go of any and all limiting ideas and experiences I have had in my relationships. I now release from my mind all thoughts of resentment, anger, irritation, contempt, arrogance, guilt, blame, codependency, rejection, abandonment, and all other negative concepts that have hampered my relationships, whether known or unknown, conscious or unconscious.

I AM now filled with positive, powerful unlimited thoughts and emotions of forgiveness, gratitude, letting go, love, calm, peacefulness, humility, respect, admiration, honor, approval, innocence, guilelessness, responsibility, acceptance, trustworthiness, and faithfulness. I AM in control of my mind and my life, now and always.

I AM now fully responsible for all of my relationships. Therefore, guilt and blame are now removed permanently from my life. I now accept fully, in consciousness, perfect harmonious relationships in my life, or better, at home and work now. I now thank God for manifesting my perfect relationships in my life, under grace, in perfect ways. I now release this prayer, fully and completely, into the Spiritual Law, knowing it does manifest, right now, in my life, under grace, in perfect ways. Thank you, God, and SO IT IS.

Overcoming Addictions and Codependency

The chains of habit are generally too small to be felt
until they are too strong to be broken.
—Samuel Johnson

There is a reason Alcoholics Anonymous is the most effective addiction treatment program available. It is because the foundation of its 12-step program is deep self-reflection and true spiritual insight. Without the help of a higher power, overcoming the gripping shackles of addiction is nearly impossible.

At first, mind-altering substances or habits appear harmless enough. Users rationalize that they can stop anytime. That is, until it is too late and the habit has devoured their lives and led them to utter ruin. This can apply to drugs, alcohol, cigarettes, sex, pornography, television, Internet, codependent relationships, gambling, work, coffee, food, sugar, or any other habit or craving.

In many cases, addictive dependency is a result of psychic over-sensitivity, explained as "Psychic Sponge Syndrome" on page 19. Wide open to acute emotions, feelings, sensations, and environmental stimuli, ultra-sensitive psychic sponges inhabit a world of stinging emotions and sensory overload whose intensity falls anywhere between mild irritation and intense terror. A poor way to cope is to bury oneself in numbing agents that temporarily remove the pain.

There is hope for such seemingly hopeless situations. With the healing prayers in this chapter, plus the self-authority prayers in Chapter 1, along with a proven recovery program, addiction and codependency can be overcome.

42. Overcoming Hypersensitivity

This prayer can reverse the tendency toward hypersensitivity. Use it anytime you feel drained, overcome, shaken, or distraught by circumstances out of your control. When your world appears to be falling apart, when it seems impossible to get a grip on reality, this prayer can help.

I AM in control.
I AM filled with the light of God.
I allow that light to fill and engulf me now.
The light of God vibrates and radiates
Within me and all around me.

That light brings adamantine invincibility.
I AM a rock, a pillar of strength.
For the strength of God's power
Is within me, and at my command.
Nothing and no one can shake
My immovable center of being.
I stand steadfast and sure in God's love.
I AM a radiant being of light,
Filled with the glory that is God.
Thank you, God, and SO IT IS.

43. Attaining and Maintaining Balance

When you restore balance in your mind, body, and spirit, it is easier to overcome addiction. Use this prayer when you feel off-kilter and need to center yourself, when you feel lost and confused amidst conflicting messages, or when your environment seems to be closing in on you.

My mind is in balance.
My body is in balance.
My spirit is in balance.
I AM filled with equanimity, equilibrium,
Stability, moderation, inner strength,
Composure, assuredness, and divine wisdom.
I make wise, decisive, and purposeful choices.
I AM the only authority in my life.
I AM divinely protected, guided, and inspired.
My life is on track, resolute, and meaningful.
I AM in control of my life and my mind.
I AM in balance,
Now and forevermore.
Thank you, God, and SO IT IS.

44. Overcoming Overwhelm

When you let go and give over all of your concerns to God, then a great burden is lifted, and you are in God's hands.

I now let go and let God
Handle all of my affairs.
All of my concerns, worries, and doubts
Are now lifted into the light
Of God's love and truth.

I hand over everything to the divine,
Knowing my life is in the hands of God.
Thank you, God, and SO IT IS.

45. Overcoming Addictive Behavior

When used several times a day, this prayer can help you overcome addiction and prevent the lure of further addictive behaviors. Whenever you feel weak, unsure of yourself, and cannot trust yourself, use this prayer.

There is nothing in this world that can possess me.
There is nothing that has control over me.
My life belongs to my Self alone.
I do not belong to anyone or anything other than my Self.
I AM not a victim, because nothing is a predator.
No substance, thing, or person is stalking me.
I have choice. In every moment, I have choice.
I now make wise and purposeful decisions.
I AM no longer consumed by addiction.
I AM no longer compelled to do anything.
I now take command of my mind and my life.
I AM in control. I AM the only authority in my life.
I answer to no one and nothing other than God within me.
God supports me in building constructive, healthy habits.
With God as my guide and my lighthouse,
I walk the path of righteousness.
God leads me on the right path to glory.
I AM led by Spirit, now and forevermore.
Thank you, God, and SO IT IS.

46. Overcoming Cigarette Addiction

Though cigarettes are a virulent addiction, you can overcome and reverse this deadly habit. Use this affirmation several times a day, any time you crave nicotine or feel a longing to smoke.

I AM filled with the breath of life.
Any seeming death wish is now banished
And released into the light of God
And it is gone.
My only desire is to embrace life and to live it.
I now know my lungs are filled with life.

I breathe in life with every breath I take.
I welcome life into my life.
I AM filled with the will to live a long life.
I AM filled with the joy of life.
Life and robust health fill every pore of my body.
I AM healthy, strong, and free,
Just as God has meant me to be.
Thank you, God, and SO IT IS.

47. Overcoming Alcoholism

This prayer can help you overcome and conquer the demon of alcoholism and its shame of secrecy. Use it many times a day, whenever the craving for alcohol tugs at you, or whenever you feel alcohol is ruling your life.

I AM free from any seeming need to drink alcohol.
With the power of God, I now overcome this craving.
With God by my side, I AM free to be my Self.
I AM free to live a healthy lifestyle.
I AM no longer a slave to alcohol.
I now break the shackles of alcoholism.
Alcohol no longer has its grip on my life.
All psychic ties between myself and alcohol
Are now lovingly cut, cut, cut, cut, cut, cut, cut, cut, cut,
Cut, cut, cut, severed, blessed, healed, lifted, released
And let go, into the light of God's love and truth.
I no longer feel the need
To cover up emotional pain and frustration.
I now know it is okay be vulnerable.
I no longer need
To cover up self-hatred and shame.
I now stand tall and confident,
Knowing I AM good enough just as I AM.
My life is my own. My life no longer belongs to alcohol.
My life now belongs to me. I AM free.
Thank you, God, and SO IT IS.

48. Overcoming Drug Addiction

Drug addiction is a wide-open invitation for lower energies and entities to invade the body. Therefore, healing lower energies is essential to overcoming addiction. Use this prayer several time a day, to help you overcome the consuming need for drugs, and to heal and release the damaging forces that have swallowed your life.

I AM in control of my life.
No substance or drug can control me.
With God's help, I AM free from addiction.
I now call upon the Holy Spirit
To cut any and all psychic ties
Between [name of substance] *and me now.*
These psychic ties are now lovingly
Cut, cut, cut, cut, cut, cut, cut, cut, cut, cut, cut,
[Repeat until it feels complete]
Severed, lifted, loved, healed, blessed, released,
And let go, into the light of God's love and truth.
I AM now free from drug addiction.
I AM filled with the light of God.
I now overcome the need to use drugs.
All craving for drugs is healed, loosed,
Lifted, loved, released, and let go now.
I AM free from all shackles that have bound me.
I AM free to move away from the darkness
And embrace the light.
All dark energies around me are now lovingly
Healed and forgiven, lifted into the light,
Healed and forgiven, lifted into the light,
[Repeat until it feels complete]
Blessed, forgiven, released and let go
Into the love, light, and wholeness of God.
I AM in control of my mind and my life now.
I AM free from dependency, free to be me.
Right here and right now.
Thank you, God, and SO IT IS.

49. Overcoming Caffeine, Sugar, Stimulants, and Narcotics

This prayer can help you overcome dependencies on stimulants, narcotics, and other quick fixes that have long-range deleterious effects. Use this prayer any time you feel the need for a stimulant to keep you going or a drug to calm you down.

I AM now free and open to positive change.
My life is free from any and all dependency.
I no longer feel the need for caffeine, sugar,
Or any other stimulant, craving, or addiction.
I no longer require stimulants to get me going.
I AM now alert and awake without substances.
I no longer need narcotics to relax me.
I AM calm and content right here and now.
I no longer require energy boosters.
I AM now filled with natural robust energy.
I no longer need artificial substances,
For I AM now my Self—simple and natural,
Just as God intended me to be.
Thank you, God, and SO IT IS.

50. Treatment for Overcoming Substance Abuse and Addiction

This is a treatment for myself, [*full name*], for overcoming all seeming substance abuse and addiction, or better, now.

I now know and recognize there is one healing power and one healing presence at work in the universe and in my life: God the good, the omnipotent. God, the source of life, gives life and sustains life in all beings. God is the light of life, the truth of being. God is unconditional love. God is perfect forgiveness, freedom, divine grace, and fulfillment. God is perfect mercy and compassion, free from judgment and blame. God is the miracle-making power. God is wholeness and oneness.

I AM now one with God, merged and unified with God in perfect alignment, harmony, and wholeness. God is right here, right now, within me—the very essence and center of my being. I AM the healing presence and power that God is. I AM one with the source of life, which gives life and sustains all beings. I AM the light of life, the truth of being. I AM unconditional love, forgiveness, freedom, grace, and fulfillment. I AM the miracle-making power that God is. I AM wholeness and oneness.

I now therefore claim for myself, [*full name*], complete and permanent freedom from any and all seeming appearance of substance abuse and addiction, or better, now.

I now know that I embrace life. I no longer harbor any death wish. Whatever seeming wrongs or harm I have caused myself or another, in this life or any past life, I now forgive and release. They are burned in the fire of divine forgiveness. I now forgive myself completely. For I have done the very best I could do in every situation, according to my level of consciousness at the time. Therefore, there is no guilt or blame. There is no need to punish or harm myself with substance abuse. For the Lord my God is with me wherever I go, and God forgives me utterly and completely, with perfect mercy and compassion.

However depraved I feel, whatever self-loathing I have harbored—all is now healed and forgiven. However I have seemingly failed, however I have abused myself and others, whatever seeming injuries, crimes, or damage I have done that has made me hate myself—all is now healed and forgiven. No matter what heinous things I have done or what good I have failed to do—I now know God loves me anyway, and I AM completely forgiven.

I now let go of any and all limiting thoughts and emotions that no longer serve me. I now release feelings of self-hatred, self-deprecation, self-abuse, self-accusation, self-condemnation, self-punishment, and self-annihilation. These thoughts are now lifted into the light of God, lifted into the light of God, and they are gone. They are burned in the fire of divine love. I now welcome and embrace new, positive thoughts and emotions of self-love, self-acceptance, self-worth, self-value, kindness and compassion toward self, forgiveness of self, unconditional love toward self, and embracing life.

I no longer turn away from life or emotions. I no longer feel the need to escape the acute pain, hurt, sorrow, desolation, and loss that life inevitably brings. I now allow life to be lived, with all its emotions. I no longer feel the need to hide or escape in substance abuse. I now welcome and embrace life. I accept all emotions and feel them without suppressing them. I AM free to experience all that life has to offer, whether pleasure, pain, happiness, or sadness.

I now cut any and all psychic ties and karmic bonds between myself and any substances that have bound me to addiction. These psychic ties are all now lovingly cut, cut, cut, cut, cut, cut, cut, cut, cut, cut, cut, cut, cut, cut, cut, cut, cut, cut, cut, severed, severed, severed, lifted, loved, healed, blessed, released, and completely let go, into the light of God's perfect love.

I AM free from any and all bondage to substance abuse. Substances no longer control me. I AM in control. I AM the only authority in my life. I AM divinely protected by the light of my being. I now close off my aura and body of light to addictive substances, and to all but my own inner divinity. I now live in perfect self-mastery, self-love, and self-acceptance. I AM awake, alert, and in control of my life and my mind, now and forevermore.

I now fully accept, in consciousness, my complete and permanent freedom from any and all seeming appearance of substance abuse or addiction, or better, now. I now thank God for manifesting this healing in my life, under grace, in perfect ways. SO BE IT.

51. Treatment for Overcoming Gambling Addiction

This is a treatment for myself, [*full name*], for overcoming any seeming appearance of gambling addiction, or better, now.

I now recognize that God is unconditional love. God is the all-loving, all-powerful, all-embracing, all-encompassing, all-compassionate, all-merciful power and presence at work in the universe. God is the perfect consummate healer. God is perfect forgiveness, kindness, care, and solace. God is the comforter.

I AM now the perfect unconditional love that God is. I AM one with the all-loving, all-powerful, all-embracing, all-encompassing, all-compassionate, all-merciful power and presence of God. I AM one with God's perfect healing power. I AM one with God's perfect forgiveness, kindness, care, and solace. I AM the comforter that God is.

I therefore know and claim, right here and now, my complete overcoming of any seeming appearance of gambling addiction, or better, now.

I now let go of all seeming addiction that has bound me. I now call upon the Holy Spirit, the spirit of truth, wholeness, and oneness, to release from my mind all trace of seeming addiction now. I now cut any and all psychic ties between myself and all gambling addiction now. These psychic ties are now lovingly cut, cut, cut, cut, cut, cut, cut, cut, cut, cut, cut, cut, cut, cut, cut, cut, cut, cut, cut cut, lifted, blessed, healed, released, dissolved, and let go. They are now burned in the fire of God's love and peace.

I AM now forgiven unconditionally for all seeming gambling addiction. I now welcome, accept, and imbibe perfect new positive thoughts and emotions of self-authority, self-love, self-confidence, self-esteem, self-value, self-worth, self-empowerment, and self-accountability now. I AM in control of my mind and my life. I AM the only authority in my life. I AM divinely protected by the light of my being. I close off my aura and body of light to all gambling now, and to all but my own inner divinity.

I now forgive myself for any and all seeming damage I have caused my loved ones as a result of gambling addiction. I now let go of all guilt and shame, and it is gone. It is released into the light of God's love. God within me is my forgiving and releasing power. God within my loved ones is their forgiving and releasing power. God within me is my forgiving and releasing power. God within my loved ones is their forgiving and releasing power. All is healed and forgiven and cleared up between us, right here and now.

I now fully accept, in consciousness, my perfect, complete overcoming of any seeming appearance of gambling addiction, or better, now. I now thank God for manifesting this perfect healing from addiction now. I now release this prayer completely into the Spiritual Law, knowing it is done as spoken, or better, now. Thank you, God, and SO BE IT.

52. Treatment for Overcoming Sex Addiction

This is a treatment for myself, [*full name*], my perfect healing of the seeming appearance of sex addiction in my life now and forevermore.

I now know and recognize that God is the only power and presence at work in the universe and in my life. God is freedom. God is healing and wholeness. God is contentment and peace. God is the light of life, the truth of being. God is divine love, forgiveness, mercy, and compassion. God is the divine healer. God is divine discernment.

I AM merged with, perfectly aligned with, and one with God. In God I live, move, and have my being. I AM a divine being of great love, light, presence, power, and glory. God lives within me, as me, in perfect alignment and harmony. I AM the love, the presence, and the power that God is. I AM God's peace, freedom, forgiveness, mercy, and compassion. I AM the healing power that God is. I AM divine discernment.

I now therefore claim for myself, [*full name*], my perfect healing of the seeming appearance of sex addiction in my life, or better, now and forevermore.

I now know with perfect certainty that I forgive myself for any and all wrongdoing I have seemingly inflicted on others. I know that no matter how much guilt and shame I feel, God's love is unconditional. Therefore, even though I have seemingly wronged others, I know God's merciful grace and compassion pours over me right now and washes me clean in the pure fountain of unconditional love. I now know God's love is more powerful than any addiction. With God, all things are possible. Therefore I know that I change my life right here and now. I now live completely free from sex addiction.

I now cut any and all psychic ties between myself and all those who have been seemingly victimized by my past harmful actions. Those psychic ties are all now lovingly cut, cut, cut, cut, cut, cut, cut, cut, cut, cut, cut, cut, cut, cut, cut, severed, healed, lifted, loved, blessed and completely let go. They are burned in the fire of God's love. I AM in control. I AM the only authority in my life. I close off my aura and body of light to the seeming victims of my past actions, and to all but my own inner divinity.

I now let go of the past, knowing I move forward with confidence. I know that whatever seeming wrong I have done, I forgive myself completely now. No matter how hard it seems to forgive myself, I now know, with God's help, I completely let go of shame, and I forgive myself now. I no longer feel the need to use and abuse others for sexual gratification. I know now I AM content within myself, for God is my protector and my guide. I no longer feel the need to harm anyone for any reason. I AM healed and forgiven, and I walk in harmony with myself and with natural law. I now attune to the laws of nature and I walk a path of balance, peace, and harmony.

I now fully accept, in consciousness, that I AM free from sex addiction now. I now release this prayer into the Spiritual Law of perfection everywhere now. Thank you, God, and SO IT IS.

53. Treatment for Freedom From Codependency

This is a treatment for myself, [*full name*], for complete freedom from codependent relationships, or better, now.

I now know and recognize there is one presence and one power at work in the universe and in my life: God the good, the omnipotent. God is the light of life, the truth of being. God is the all-loving, all-embracing, all-powerful, and all-encompassing. God is unconditional love, harmony, peace, and tranquility. God is the divine healer. God is the perfection of being—perfection everywhere now. God is freedom, independence, self-containment, self-empowerment, and utter contentment.

I AM now one with God, perfect and whole in unity. God dwells within me, as me, in perfect harmony and tranquility. I AM the unconditional love and healing presence that God is. I AM pure love, as God is. I AM now filled and surrounded with God's perfect peace, freedom, independence, self-containment, self-empowerment, and total contentment. God's love fills my heart. God's light surrounds me. I AM a divine being of great power and glory.

I now therefore claim for myself, [*full name*], complete freedom from codependent relationships, or better, now.

I now let go of any and all seeming need to lose myself in any other person. I now cut any and all psychic ties, karmic bonds, binding ties, and unhealthy connections between myself and all codependent relationships now. I now let go of any seeming need for psychic bondage. These psychic ties are now lovingly cut, cut, cut, cut, cut, cut, cut, cut, cut, cut, cut, lifted, loved, healed, severed, released, blessed, and let go into the light of God's love and truth. I no longer feel the need to cling to others. I no longer possess another. I AM in possession of my Self alone now. I AM free now.

I now let go of any and all negative, limiting thoughts and emotions that no longer serve me. I now release from my mind all self-hatred, self-effacement, self-destruction, possessiveness, jealousy, clinging, domination, coercion, manipulation, vampirism, and any other codependent mental tendencies and behaviors now, whether conscious or unconscious, known or unknown.

I now welcome and accept new, positive, life-affirming thoughts and emotions of self-empowerment, self-love, self-acceptance, self-worth, self-confidence, freedom, independence, autonomy, inner strength, permissiveness, tolerance, acceptance, and all other tendencies that support a life free from dependency now.

I AM in control. I AM the only authority in my life. I AM divinely protected by the light of my being. I close off my aura and body of light to all those who are unduly influencing me, and to all those with whom I have had codependent relationships. I AM in touch with my Self, and I now know my worth and value. I AM worthy to love and be loved in freedom, without any seeming need for codependency.

I now thank God for manifesting this healing in my life, under grace, in perfect ways. I now release this prayer into the Spiritual Law, knowing it demonstrates right now in my life, under God's grace, in perfect ways. Thank you, God, and SO IT IS.

54. Treatment for Overcoming Workaholism

This is a treatment for myself, [*full name*], for overcoming all seeming workaholism, or better, now.

I now recognize that there is one power and one presence in my life. That presence is God. I recognize that God is perfect peace. God's peace is within everyone and everything. God is serenity, tranquility, and perfect contentment. God is balance, harmony, equilibrium, and equanimity. God is love.

I AM now one with God. In God, I live, move, breathe, and have my being. God and I are one, in perfect harmony. I AM merged with, aligned with, and the same as God. I AM one with God in perfect seamless wholeness. God's love and peace dwell within me. At the center of my being, there God is. I AM the perfect balance, harmony, equilibrium, and equanimity that God is. All that God is, I AM.

I therefore now know and claim for myself, [*full name*], perfect freedom from all seeming workaholism, or better, now.

I no longer feel the need to use work as an escape from feeling emotions. I now release from my mind any and all thoughts and feelings that no longer serve me. I now let go of the seeming need to suppress emotions.

I release from my mind all fear, guilt, shame, unworthiness, sadness, anger, frustration, lack, emptiness, and pain. All these thoughts are lifted, loved, healed, released, blessed, and let go, into the light of God's love and truth.

I now welcome and accept new, beautiful, creative thoughts and emotions of faith, trust, patience, forgiveness, confidence, self-worth, self-love, happiness, peace, contentment, fullness, fulfillment, joy, freedom, and comfort. I AM in control of my mind and my life, now and forevermore.

I now know it is acceptable to feel emotions. I no longer feel the need to wear a mask of perfectionism. I now allow myself to be myself. I no longer judge myself. I accept myself exactly as I AM, knowing I AM perfect in every way, just as I AM. I now find value in myself. I no longer gauge my value based solely on work accomplishments. I AM valuable just being myself. I AM enough, just as I AM, right here and now. I now accept and welcome love and friendship into my life, and I no longer feel the seeming need to use work as a way to escape being hurt in relationships.

I now release, loose, and let go of any and all relationships from my past that have caused pain. I now cut any and all psychic ties, negative connections, and karmic bonds between myself and all those who have seemingly hurt me. These psychic ties are now lovingly cut, cut, cut, cut, cut, cut, cut, cut, cut, healed, dissolved, loved, lifted, released, blessed, and let go. I AM free from these ties, and I now move on with my life, as I let them go. I AM in control of my mind and my life. I AM free.

I fully accept, in consciousness, complete healing of seeming workaholism now. I now release and let go of this prayer into the Spiritual Law, which is at work now, manifesting it into my life, in perfect ways. I fully accept the action of the Spiritual Law. Thank you, God, and SO IT IS.

55. Treatment for Overcoming Food Addiction

This is a treatment for myself, [*full name*], for overcoming all seeming food addiction, or better, now.

I now recognize that God is the one power and one presence in the universe and in my life. God is the all-loving, all-embracing, all-encompassing, all-powerful presence that pervades and permeates the universe. God's unconditional love is everywhere present, within everyone and everything. God is wholeness, oneness, fullness, and fulfillment. God is total contentment and inner peace. God is perfection everywhere now. God is perfection here now.

I AM now one with, attuned with, aligned with, and one with God, in a perfect seamless wholeness. In God I live, move, and have my being. God is within me and all around me. God's all-loving, all-embracing, all-encompassing, all-powerful presence pervades and permeates me. I AM the unconditional love that God is, present in the center of my being. I AM the wholeness, oneness, fullness, and fulfillment that God is. I AM total contentment and inner peace. I AM perfection everywhere now. I AM perfection here now.

I now therefore know and claim for myself, [*full name*], the perfect healing of any and all seeming food addiction, or better, now.

I release from my mind any and all seeming food addiction now. I now call upon the Holy Spirit, the Spirit of truth and wholeness, to shine the light of truth upon my mind now. I now release, loose, and let go of all thoughts and emotions of lack, limitation, frustration, fear, self-destruction, self-hatred, guilt, anger, sadness, pain, resentment, and rejection now.

I now welcome and embrace thoughts of fullness, fulfillment, limitlessness, inner peace, contentment, faith, trust, self-love, self-acceptance, forgiveness, joy, comfort, gratitude, love of life, enthusiasm, inspiration, and happiness now.

I now release from my mind all concepts of self-image that do not reflect the truth of my being. I release all ideas of being fat, obese, ugly, unattractive, and sexually unappealing now. I now welcome and accept that I AM slender, beautiful, handsome, attractive, and sexually appealing. My body is slender, sexy, and attractive.

I now release any and all seeming obsession to clean my plate. I now let go of any and all fallacy and superstition that I must clean my plate because people are starving in a foreign country. No matter how much food is on my plate, I now eat as much as I need, and I leave the rest. It is not sinful to leave food on the plate. It is better for food to become garbage than for my body to become a human garbage can. The waste can either show up on my body, or it can become garbage. I choose for the waste to become garbage now.

I now let go of the idea that there is not enough in my life. There is enough, and I AM enough. I do not need to fill emptiness in my life with food. My life is full, whole, and complete, exactly as it is. My life is good enough, right now. I AM enough, right now. I AM full. I AM full with divine love, joy, friendship, happiness, fulfillment, and contentment now. I AM in control of my mind and my life, right here and now. I AM fully content, whole, and complete, right here and now.

I now fully accept, in consciousness, that I AM free from any and all seeming food addiction, or better, now. I now thank God for manifesting this healing now, in my life, under God's grace, in God's own wise and perfect ways. I now release this prayer into the light of God, knowing it does manifest right now. I thank God that this is so now, and SO IT IS.

Dispelling Illusions and False Perceptions

If the doors of perception were cleansed, everything would appear to man as it is, infinite.
—William Blake

Have you ever considered that what you believe to be truth is not really truth? Your perception of reality might be skewed by false beliefs, habits, conditions, and patterns. Voices of parents, teachers, family, friends, peers, coworkers, pastors, rabbis, priests, gurus, psychics, doctors, psychologists, counselors, society, the media, and the collective human consciousness have all brainwashed you to believe as you do.

Therefore, how you perceive yourself is colored by the window through which you gaze. That window might be clear, pristine, and colorless, or any color in the rainbow. Who you think you are is not who you really are. For you are bound by illusions and false perceptions. Even the great saint on the mountaintop has a body, and anyone dwelling in physical form is, by definition, in *avidya* (ignorance), or at the very least *lesh avidya* (faint remains of ignorance).

In this chapter, you are invited to let go of some illusory perceptions that have been held as mental laws, and you can create new laws closer to the truth: "For now we see through a glass, darkly; but then face to face: now I know in part; but then shall I know even as also I am known." (1 Corinthians 13:12)

56. Mental Law Healing Prayer

Your life is governed by laws created in your mind, a set of beliefs you have accepted as truth. These laws, both conscious and unconscious, determine your life experiences and destiny. Once these personal mental laws have been established, their limiting statutes are difficult to reverse. However, with the power of prayer, every law can be rewritten.

Now let us do an exercise. Take out a piece of paper. Pretend you have an empty slate on which to write your destiny. On the left side of the paper, write the mental laws by which you have been governed so far. On the right side, write a set of laws by which you would like to be governed. Your slate may look something like this:

My Personal Mental Laws	
Laws I Have Experienced	Laws I Would Like
I rarely get what I want.	I always get what I want.
I never have enough money.	I always have all the money I need.
I am not very happy.	I am a very happy person.
I have very few friends.	I have a lot of friends.
I hate my work.	I love my work.
I have a difficult family.	I have a harmonious family.
I am socially uncomfortable.	I feel at ease in social situations.
I can't lose weight.	I am slim and trim.
I can't see without glasses.	I have perfect eyesight.
I have no love in my life.	I have a wonderful love relationship.

Now let us release the negative metal laws and accept new, positive mental laws. Read the following prayer aloud. When you come to the first prompt, read the "Laws I Have Experienced" list in the left column of your paper When you come to the second prompt, read the "Laws I Would Like" list in the right column of your paper.

I call upon the Holy Spirit to lovingly, fully, and completely
Heal and release all limiting mental laws that no longer serve me,
That have governed my life, and have affected me adversely.
These error-beliefs are now filled with
Divine love, divine light, and divine truth.
I now release, loose, and let go from my mind
All mental laws of [list the negative mental laws here].
They are lifted into the light of truth,
Dissolved into the nothingness of what they truly are,
Burned in the fire of God's love, and they are gone.
I now accept mental laws that nourish my life
In powerful, positive ways.
I now welcome new, creative, uplifting,
Inspiring, joyful mental laws of
[List the positive mental laws here].
I now thank God for manifesting this good in my life,
Under grace, in powerful, positive, perfect ways.
Thank you, wonderful God, and SO IT IS.

57. Dispelling False Responsibility

False responsibility occurs when people's sense of self-worth is directly proportional to how much they imagine they are saving or rescuing others. Bound to others' problems, such people neglect themselves and become drained and exhausted. However, the best way to help and serve others is to build your own inner strength.

I AM filled with such divine peace, content, and grace
That I need nothing other than this to feel whole.
I AM perfect, complete, and whole, exactly as I AM.
I AM responsible to my Self and to God within me.
I now let go of the need to save everyone else.
My self-worth and value are no longer determined
By how virtuously, righteously, and piously I act.
I now know and accept that I AM worthy and valuable
No matter what I do, or do not do.
I release any and all seeming addiction
To absorbing illness, misery, and challenges of others.
I now honor, respect, value, and care for
My own body, mind, soul, and Spirit.
I AM now my own number-one priority.
I AM now worthy to receive nurturing, love,
Compassion, healing, and sustenance.
I no longer feel the need to earn love.
I know God's love is freely given, and I do receive it now.
I now welcome love into my life. I AM loved.
Thank you, God, and SO IT IS.

58. Reversing Enabling Behavior

Addictive behavior affects all those around addicts: family, friends, and coworkers. Addicts cannot be cured if loved ones ignore the problem, tolerate abusive behavior, or let the habit continue without intervention. *Enablers* are defined as those who enable addicts to continue their addiction.

I now know God's strength is within and all around me.
God's divine power resides within my heart,
And gives me the strength and courage
To love, honor, cherish, and respect others
Without enabling any of their addictions.
My discerning eye now knows what is for the good of all.

I now know that passively allowing or supporting
Other people's addictions does not serve anyone.
I now know I have the courage and strength
To stand my ground and to say no.
I no longer support or encourage addictive behavior.
I AM my own number-one priority now.
I now love, nurture, cherish, and protect myself.
I no longer allow an addict to control me.
I AM in control of my mind and my life.
I AM the only authority in my life.
I AM divinely protected by the light of my being.
Thank you, God, and SO IT IS.

59. Dismissing Superiority and Inferiority

God shines its light and sends the rain on everyone and everything, without discrimination, prejudice, or condemnation. We as humans would do well to emulate God's vision, the all-seeing eye that sees everyone equally.

There is no higher or lower, no more than or less than;
For all are equal in the sight of God.
No one is superior or inferior; no one is better or worse;
For all are created in the perfect likeness and image of God.
There is no this or that, no black or white;
For all is one, unified and whole.
There is no up or down, no right or left;
For there is only one life, one light, and one truth.
That oneness is all that is.
That oneness is all that I AM.
That oneness is the truth of my being.
That oneness is the truth of being of all.
No one and nothing is separate from that oneness.
All is that oneness.
All that God is, I AM, as are all.
All that I AM, God is, as are all.

60. Overcoming Spiritual Gullibility

A great problem in the spiritual field is the tendency to trust those who are untrustworthy. Though sensitive and intuitive, spiritual seekers often have a seeming blind spot preventing them from discernment when choosing spiritual teachers who make impossible claims.

I now stand in the truth of God. I stand in the truth of being.
I AM in control of my mind and my life.
I AM the only authority in my life.
I AM a mighty, powerful, divine spiritual being.
I AM a being of great wisdom and discernment.
I now dispel, let go, and release from my mind
Any and all spiritual gullibility and psychic deception.
I now call upon the Holy Spirit to bless me and grant me
The gifts of divine discrimination and discernment.
I AM as wise, shrewd, and astute as a serpent,
Yet harmless, guileless, and innocent as a dove.
I no longer ignore the body signals that show me
When something or someone is amiss.
I now pay attention to what the body is saying.
I now let go of any tendency to indiscriminately accept
Psychic manipulation, coercion, or exploitation.
I no longer naively believe, without testing or investigation,
Any gurus, psychics, diviners, fortune-tellers, astrologers,
Religious or spiritual leaders, or other authority figures
Who make ridiculous promises and absurd claims,
Who speak and act pretentiously, with vanity and affectation,
With self-importance, arrogance, and false humility.
I now notice and trust my God-given intuition,
Which shows me warning signs, red flags, and alarms.
I now trust my higher Self and inner divinity
More than flashy, ostentatious orations and shows
Of fame, celebrity, status, charm, or mystique,
Of false, misleading pretensions of so-called wisdom.
I no longer trust the façade. I now perceive the truth.
I now recognize, with God's perfect eye of discernment,
Who is genuine and sincere, who is deluded and misled,
Who is hoodwinking or deceiving others,
And who is using others as pawns in their game.
I now see, know, feel, and sense the truth.
I welcome and embrace only the truth right now.
Thank you, God, and SO IT IS.

61. Eliminating Spiritual Elitism

Some spiritual and religious people, cult members, environmentalists, liberal humanists, volunteers, and other idealists imagine themselves highly superior to the *hoi polloi*. Regrettably, spiritual elitism appears to come with the territory of spiritual organizations.

My spiritual path is the path I have chosen,
Through my own free-will choice.
My path is no less than or greater than any other.
My ideal of spirituality is no higher or lower than another's.
My dream of God is no greater or less than another's.
My sense of self-worth is no longer determined
By how spiritual I imagine myself to be.
I now embrace all beings as true spiritual brothers and sisters.
I AM free from spiritual superiority and spiritual egotism.
All elitism, haughtiness, arrogance, condescension,
Disdain, derision, and contempt are released from my mind.
They are now dispelled, dissolved, and completely let go.
They are lifted into the light of God's love and truth.
I now welcome and fully embrace humility, appreciation,
Respect, unpretentiousness, gratitude, kindness, gentleness,
Guilelessness, innocence, and unconditional love.
I now claim, know, and fully accept with certainty
That all people on this planet,
No matter what path they walk or religion they follow,
Are divine, mighty, powerful spiritual beings,
Walking their perfect path in the perfect way.
For all are created in the likeness and image of God.
All are one light, one presence, one divine intelligence,
One love, one truth, and one perfection of being.
I AM free from spiritual elitism, now and forevermore.
Thank you, God, and SO IT IS.

62. Overcoming Spiritual Materialism

When people bring values of materialism into their spiritual life, then problems of a material nature follow them. Arrogance, haughtiness, egotism, jealousy, rank, pretentiousness, and craving for fame can lead spiritual seekers astray from their true spiritual path. This prayer can help.

God's love fills my heart. God's light surrounds me.
God's peace dwells within me. God's presence guides me.
God is my only guide. God is my way of being.
I have no idol and worship no master.
My ego identity is not bound
By imagined measurements of spirituality.
I no longer judge or separate myself or others
Based upon erroneous, false standards
Of piety, religious fervor, zealousness,
Or any other yardstick of religious idealism.
I now release from my mind all narcissistic,
Self-important, ego-inflated, pompous, pretentious,
False valuations that magnify or separate myself from others.
I AM now unimpressed by fame, celebrity, money,
By education, love, beauty, rank, office, or status.
I accept myself as perfect, and I accept all as perfect.
All are divine beings, equal in the sight of God.
There is no spiritual standard or comparison
That ranks or grades anyone higher, lower, better, or worse.
I AM one with my Self, one with God, and one with all beings.
Thank you, God, and SO IT IS.

63. Overcoming Guilt and Shame

Carrying around guilt and shame is a nearly universal sickness today. Whatever you focus on manifests in your life, so if you continually focus on guilt, penalty, and retribution, then you will attract punishment into your life.

I AM filled with the light of God.
I AM unified with the truth of my being.
I AM a divine being of inner strength,
Power, light, love, energy, and wisdom.
No matter what I have ever done
Or how harshly I have judged myself,
I now know God loves me unconditionally,
God is the all-merciful forgiving power, the comforter,
The all-compassionate, all-understanding light of my life.
All seeming guilt and shame that I have carried
In my mind and emotions, from this life,

And from any past lives, is now lovingly
Healed, blessed, dissolved, loosed, released, and let go,
Lifted into the light of God—and it is gone.
I now forgive myself fully and completely,
Knowing I have done the very best I could do,
In every situation and circumstance,
According to my level of consciousness at the time.
Therefore I know I AM free from guilt and shame.
I like myself, I love myself, I accept myself,
Exactly as I AM—perfect, complete, and whole.
Thank you, God, and SO IT IS.

64. Dispelling Spiritual Illusion

This prayer can help you identify who you really are, and define who or what you are not. Saying this prayer often can help you realize your spiritual awakening.

I AM the immortal, pure, stainless, immeasurable,
Nameless, formless, infinite, eternal, imperishable,
Unmanifest, unborn, undying, unbounded, unlimited
Divine being—absolute pure consciousness.
I now wake up from the dream of my Self as ego.
I now release from my mind any and all ideas,
Concepts, patterns, habits, and constructs of my Self
As anything other than the immortal absolute.
I now let go of the idea of who I think I am.
I no longer identify my Self as body, age, health, ego,
Name, status, position, job, education, assets, possessions,
Religion, spiritual attainment, intelligence, personality,
Sense of humor, hobbies, addictions, accomplishments,
Ego, machismo, feminism, self-image, perfectionism,
Superiority, inferiority, and any other construct of myself,
Whether known or unknown, conscious or unconscious.
I now accept and welcome the truth about my Self.
I now realize who I really AM.
I AM That. Thou art That. All this is That. That alone is.
Thank you, God, and SO IT IS.

65. Treatment for Spiritual Discernment

This is a treatment for myself, [*full name*], for perfect spiritual discernment, or better, now.

I now know and recognize there is one power and one presence in the universe and in my life: God the good, omnipotent, omnipresent, omniscient, with perfect wisdom. God is the lighthouse of life, the divine inner teacher and wayshower. God is the straight and narrow road that leads to perfection. God is the light that illumines the pathway. God is perfection everywhere now. God is perfection here now.

I AM now one with the power and the presence of God. I AM now one with God's good, with God's omnipotence, omnipresence, omniscience, and perfect wisdom now. I now follow the straight and narrow inner pathway that leads to perfection, as God shows me the way from within. I AM one with the lighthouse of life, God's light, which illumines the pathway. I AM perfection everywhere now. I AM perfection here now.

I now therefore know and claim for myself, [*full name*], my perfect spiritual discernment, or better, now.

I now release from my mind any and all thoughts, feelings, and emotions that have clouded my mind and caused me confusion. I now let go of any and all thoughts of gullibility, poor choices, error-judgments, ignorance, indiscrimination, unawareness, contracted consciousness, confusion, uncertainty, foolishness, rejection, missed opportunities, and lack of trust in God. These thoughts are now lifted, healed, released, and let go, and they are gone. They are burned in the divine fire of discernment.

I now let go of any and all tendency to be tricked, swindled, or cheated by fakers, frauds, shams, scams, and cons of this world and of the astral world. I AM in control. I AM the only authority in my life. I AM divinely protected by the light of my being. I close off my aura to all fakers, frauds, shams, scams, and cons, or better, now.

I now cut any and all psychic ties between myself and those who have duped, conned, swindled, hoodwinked, or deceived me. I close off my aura to the lower astral levels of mind. I AM in control of my mind and my life. I AM free of all swindlers and scammers now. I now walk the "razor's edge"—the pure and perfect path that leads straight to God. I no longer stumble and trip into pitfalls and hazards along the way.

I now accept and welcome into my mind and heart new, powerful, positive, wise thoughts and emotions that allow me to see and know the truth. I AM filled with thoughts of wisdom, truth, common sense, street smarts, sharp intellect, shrewdness, prudence, judiciousness, sagacity, coherence, logic, reason, and rationality, or better, now. I now know my mind is crystal clear and imbued with spiritual discernment. I open my heart to the wisdom of God, which brings me a razor-sharp intellect with perfect, clear divine insight, intuition, and discrimination.

I now accept, in consciousness, my perfect spiritual discernment, or better, now. I now thank God for manifesting into my mind perfect spiritual discernment now. I now release this claim into the Spiritual Law, which is now at work on it, and manifests it now, under God's grace and blessings. This claim now demonstrates in perfect divine order and timing, right now. Thank you, God, and SO IT IS.

Becoming All You Can Be

Make the most of yourself, for that is all there is of you.
—Ralph Waldo Emerson

When it comes to human potential, the sky is the limit. We have barely begun to explore the uncharted vast universe, or the unknown limitless regions of inner space. We know very little about what humanity is capable of. Our greatest accomplishments pale in comparison to what could be realized, with imagination and inspiration.

There are accomplished yogis who can stop and start their heart beating, survive underground in coffin-like spaces for days, generate inner heat to sustain themselves in subzero temperatures without freezing, or pierce their flesh without leaving a scar. In my book *Ascension,* I relate stories of those who have attained extraordinary longevity—even conquered death. Such feats of human mastery are but a hint of what is possible.

The prayers in this chapter can jumpstart the process of realizing your enormous human potential. With these prayers, you can begin to achieve self-mastery. You can transform your life from banality to originality, as you realize who you really are—a mighty, powerful being of unlimited capacity, unbounded creativity, and unique qualities that are a gift to the universe.

Your human potential is without limits. Let us begin to develop it now.

66. Self-Acceptance

Your first step to developing unlimited potential is self-acceptance. This prayer can help you accept yourself exactly as you are, right now.

I AM perfect, complete, and whole.
Nothing is missing from me.
I AM adequate and enough, exactly as I AM.
I AM as God created me,
Pure and flawless in every way.
I like myself, I love myself,
I accept myself, I embrace myself.
There is nothing I need to change.
I AM a one-of-a kind original—
Perfect, complete, and whole.
Thank you, God, and SO IT IS.

67. Inner Freedom

Who are you? Are you this body, or something greater—a spiritual being? This prayer will help you affirm your freedom as a perfect divine spiritual being.

I AM not this body. I AM free.
I AM as God created me to be.
I AM free, pure, full, and perfect,
Infinitely loved and loving, whole and complete.
I AM filled and surrounded with divine love.
I AM filled and surrounded with divine light.
Thank you, God, and SO IT IS.

68. Self-Expression

When you love and accept yourself, then you can be and express your true Self: "This above all: to thine own self be true, And it must follow, as the night the day, Thou canst not then be false to any man." (*Hamlet* I, iii, 78–80)

I AM now eternally sustained by the presence of God.
I need do nothing to change my already perfect being.
I now know I can be my Self,
For what I AM is already perfect, as I AM.
I no longer wear a mask to hide my Self.
Who I AM need not hide its light.
My inner light shines like the sun.
I now express who I AM in freedom.
I AM me, my Self, and I,
Natural and free, as God created me.
I AM happy to be me.
I AM free.
Thank you, God, and SO IT IS.

69. Divine Creativity

When you align yourself with God's infinite creativity, then your inner genius comes forth, and your creative expression brings success and happiness.

God is my source of unlimited strength and creative expression.
I AM the creative power in my world. I AM infinite creativity.
In God I live, move, and have my being.
In me God lives, moves, and has expression.

I now create joy, love, and success.
I now see more health, wealth, and happiness
Than I have ever seen before.
The kingdom of God within me
Is a treasure of divine ideas that enrich my life.
Thank you, God, and SO IT IS.

70. Uniting With God

As you unite with the presence that God is, you become the expression of God in this very lifetime, right now.

God is all, both visible and invisible.
One presence, one mind, one power is all.
This One, that is all, is perfect life,
Perfect love, and perfect substance.
I AM an individualized expression of God,
Ever one with this perfect life,
Perfect love, and perfect substance.
Thank you, God, and SO IT IS.

71. God Is My Priority

Making God your first priority is the best use of the precious gift of this incarnation. Love and serve God first, and your life will be meaningful and miraculous: "But seek ye first the kingdom of God, and his righteousness; and all these things shall be added unto you." (Matthew 6:33)

God is always first in my life.
I AM living a God-centered life.
God is my number-one priority.
God is the answer to my every prayer.
I AM immersed in the kingdom of God,
Today and every day.
God's inspiration is music for my soul,
God's wisdom is illumination for my mind,
God's love is comfort for my heart.
God is my way, my strength, my lighthouse.
Thank you, God, and SO IT IS.

72. Expressing God's Attributes of Mercy

In Jewish mysticism, *Mussar* is a practice of personal transformation in which spiritual values are expressed in everyday life. The attributes of God, listed in Exodus 34:6–7, are called *Middot.* This prayer can help you develop these qualities. But to really live them requires dedicated action.

I now emulate and express God's sublime attributes of mercy.
I AM the mercy and loving kindness that God is.
I AM the compassion that God is.
I AM the graciousness that God is.
I AM the patience and forbearance that God is.
I AM the kindness that God is.
I AM the faithfulness that God is.
I AM the expansion of kindness that God is.
I AM the forgiveness that God is.
I AM the justice that God is.
I now express all that God is.
Thank you, God, and SO IT IS.

73. Living in the Heart of God

When you live a life of mysticism, and you let God's energy move through you, your life takes on profound meaning and power.

I AM infinite being. I AM a radiant light-bearer.
I AM one with infinite life and wisdom.
My heart is one with the heart of God.
My mind is one with the infinite divine mind.
My body is one with God's immortal body.
The light of God shines brightly through me.
The eternal life of God lives and breathes
In me, through me, all around me, as me.
God's life, the one life, is my life now.
The pure life of God flows through me
From center to circumference, never ending.
Thank you, God, and SO IT IS.

74. Living Life as God

When you fully merge and align with God in divine oneness, that is the life worth living, the life divine. Live that life, and you will never be alone. For God is always with you, within you, and all around you.

I AM merged, immersed, aligned, attuned, and united
With the power and presence of God.
I AM a child of God. Therefore, I look like God.

I think like God. I speak like God. I act like God.
I feel like God. And I respond like God in every situation.
Every breath I take is a breath of God.
My heart beats with the heart of God.
I see the world through the eyes of God.
I hear the voice of God. I speak the words of God.
My hands do the works of God. My feet walk in God's footsteps.
I AM a walking, talking, breathing messenger of God.
I AM God in action, God in activity.
I AM God's ambassador, God's philanthropist.
I AM the spark of God in human form and human flesh.
The kingdom of God is within me.
Thank you, God, and SO IT IS.

75. Oneness Prayer

This profound prayer is a statement of the ultimate truth of life. It can help you attain spiritual enlightenment and liberation.

I AM that I AM.
All that God is, I AM.
All that I AM, God is.
I AM that I AM.
I AM That Oneness.
Thou art That Oneness.
All this is That Oneness.
That Oneness alone is.

76. Ascension Prayer

If it is your pathway to cultivate ascension in this lifetime, you can use this prayer to help you transform your physical body into a radiant light body. Read more about this in my book *Ascension.*

I AM the resurrection and the life.
I AM perfection everywhere now.
I AM perfection here now.
I AM perfect, whole, and complete.
I AM the immortal body of golden hue now.
I AM the immortal body of grace and light now.
I AM the immortal body of bliss now.
I AM the immortal rainbow body now.

I AM the ascension now.
This body is transformed into an ascended body.
I AM an ascended master now.
[Repeat at least three times.]
Thank you, God, and SO IT IS.

77. Perfection and Wholeness

God within you, at the very center of your being, is perfect, pure, and flawless. This prayer can help you realize the perfection of your being.

I AM the immaculate conception of God now.
I AM the immaculate perfection of God now.
I AM perfection everywhere now.
I AM That I AM divine perfection
I AM the divine expression of perfection:
Perfection everywhere present,
Perfection everywhere now,
Perfection here now.
I AM ever one with perfect life,
Perfect love, and perfect substance:
Whole and complete in every way.
Thank you, God, and SO IT IS.

78. Inner Wisdom

The "still small voice" within can give you guidance, wisdom, and inspiration whenever you want, at will. All you need to do is ask. Read my books *Divine Revelation* and *How to Hear the Voice of God* to learn more.

My mind is united with the mind of God.
God's perfect wisdom is within me.
I now open to the heart of God,
Where all true and genuine wisdom resides.
The ever-flowing fountainhead of divine wisdom
Is right here, inside me, accessible always.
I AM now open to that perpetual flow of wisdom,
To the "still small voice" within.
I now receive true divine guidance through
Opening my inner sight, sound, and feeling.
I continually receive divine wisdom from within.
Thank you, God, and SO IT IS.

79. God's Wisdom

Use this prayer to help you develop greater wisdom, understanding, and insight, the wisdom that comes directly from God.

God is my source of wisdom,
A wisdom that sustains and guides me always.
Peace calms my soul
As I trust God's inner wisdom to direct me.
I AM wise, for I have access to infinite wisdom within.
I AM an illumined child of God,
Filled with the spirit of divine wisdom.
I have the mind of God. I AM wise with God's wisdom.
The light of God's wisdom shines within me,
Through me, and all around me.
Thank you, God, and SO IT IS.

80. Inner Guidance

God will direct your pathway and guide your footsteps to your highest good. Just ask, and you will be led by Spirit.

I AM divinely guided in all my ways.
I trust my higher Self. I listen with love to my inner voice.
God's guidance is a message of love and caring
That resounds within my soul.
I AM led by Spirit in all I think, say, and do.
I AM always divinely guided and inspired.
I AM now led to all that is for my highest good.
I open my spiritual eyes to see all God shows me.
I open my spiritual ears to hear all God speaks to me.
God speaks to me in a gentle whisper of divine ideas.
The radiant light of God illumines my mind
And directs me in all I do.
God goes before me and prepares my way.
I always take the right turn in the road,
For God walks with me in each moment,
And God gives his angels charge over me,
To keep me in all my ways.
Thank you, God, and SO IT IS.

81. Inner Truth

God is truth, and God's truth can be expressed through you when you attune yourself to the voice of God, the presence of God, and the grace of God.

I know the truth, and the truth sets me free.
Divine understanding is the guiding light of my life.
God is showing me truth from within
Concerning all situations and circumstances now.
I AM wise and confident
Through the all-knowing presence of God.
The truth of God speaks
Through my positive, life-affirming thoughts and words.
I AM consistent and persistent
In thinking and speaking only God's truth, everyday.
Today in every situation,
I choose to bear witness to the truth
By expressing the love, life, peace, and enthusiasm of God.
Thank you, God, and SO IT IS.

82. Treatment for Self-Acceptance

This is a treatment for myself, [*full name*], for perfect self-acceptance, or better, now.

I now know and recognize there is but one life. That life is God. There is but one mind and one power. That power is God. There is but one love. That love is God. God is life that heals all, wisdom that guides all, and love that comforts all. God is pure, unconditional love, complete and whole.

There is only one life and that is God's life. That life is my life now. There is nowhere that God is not. God is right here, right now, within me and all around me. I AM merged with, united with, immersed in, and one with the presence of God. I now open my heart to the sacred presence of God, and I trust in God's enduring, sustaining, infinite love. I AM filled with unconditional love, complete and whole.

I now therefore claim for myself, [*full name*], perfect self-acceptance, or better, now.

I now let go of everything in my life that is unloving. I now release and let go of any and all negative beliefs about myself. I release from my mind and heart all thoughts and emotions of self-hatred, self-deprecation, self-destruction, self-sabotage, self-incrimination, self-punishment, and self-loathing. I now welcome and accept thoughts and emotions of self-love, self-forgiveness, self-empowerment, self-sustenance, self-acceptance, self-confidence, self-approval, self-adequacy, self-esteem, and self-worth now. I know the truth—I AM perfect, complete, and whole, created in God's likeness and image.

I accept myself unconditionally. I approve of myself unconditionally. I forgive myself unconditionally. I bless myself unconditionally. I accept myself exactly as I AM. I AM worthy of God's good for me, exactly as I AM. I AM acceptance. I AM loving, loveable, accepting, and acceptable. I AM a child of God, worthy and precious in God's eyes. I accept and cherish myself as God accepts and cherishes me. God's love fills and surrounds me with peace, blessings, grace, and comfort. I AM accepted, right now and always.

I now fully accept, in consciousness, my perfect self-acceptance, or better, now. I now thank God for manifesting this good in my life, under God's grace, in God's own wise and perfect ways, and I thank God this is so now, and SO IT IS.

83. Treatment for Overcoming Shyness

This is a treatment for myself, [*full name*], for perfect overcoming of any and all seeming shyness, or better, now.

I now know and recognize that there is one power and one presence at work in the universe and in my life: God the good, the omnipotent. God is the rock where strength and refuge are found. God is the one fortress, the one deliverer, the one redeemer. God sustains all, maintains all, and gives life to all. God is the source of life and the power that breathes life into everything and everyone.

I AM strong in the power of God's might. I AM a tower of strength and stability. Wherever God is, there strength is found. Therefore God's might and constancy fill and surround me now. I AM blessed with God's sustaining power, which brings deliverance and redemption. I AM filled with God's life-giving power, which gives courage and confidence.

I therefore now know and claim for myself, [*full name*], perfect overcoming of any and all seeming shyness, or better, now.

I now release, loose, and let go from my mind any and all seeming appearance of shyness now. I now allow myself to be my Self with perfect self-confidence and self-worth, or better, now. I now let go of any and all thoughts of timidity, shyness, shame, fear of exposure, fear of making a mistake, fear of being judged, fear of being condemned, and fear of appearing foolish. These negative thoughts are now lovingly lifted, healed, release, and completely let go, into the light of God's love and truth.

I AM now filled with new, beautiful, creative thoughts and emotions of courage, strength, friendliness, amiability, congeniality, likeability, self-confidence, self-acceptance, self-worth, self-esteem, self-respect, and self-love now.

I now know I AM perfect exactly as I AM. I do not need to hide my light. I now let my light shine in all its glory. My mind is filled with the power of God. That power is released in me, and I AM daily changed into a likeness more and more like God. God's eternal strength and glory fill and surround me with courage. I AM not moved by the opinions of others. I do not depend on others to give me a sense of value. I now know God's eternal value is established in me, giving me strength and worthiness, right here and now.

I now fully accept, in consciousness, that I now overcome any seeming appearance of shyness, or better, now. I AM filled with inner strength, self-confidence, self-worth, and self-expression, or better, now.

I now thank God for manifesting this good in my life, under God's grace, in perfect ways. I now release this prayer, fully and completely, into the Spiritual Law of Perfection Everywhere Now, knowing it is accepted and it manifests in my life right now, under grace, in perfect ways. I now thank God this is so, now, and SO IT IS.

84. Treatment for Self-Expression

This is a treatment for myself, [*full name*], for my perfect self-expression, led by the Spirit of God, or better, now.

I now recognize God is the one power and one presence that creates, maintains, and sustains the universe. God gives rise to the universe in all its manifold expressions. God fills the universe with perfect expression of love, manifested as all the forms and phenomena in the cosmos. God's universe is the expression of who and what God is—perfect, whole, and complete in every way. God is perfection everywhere now. God is perfection here now.

God is here, there, and everywhere, in this, that, and everything. Therefore, I AM now one with, merged with, aligned with, and immersed in the presence of God. In God I live, move, and have my being. God is within and all around me. I AM the expression of God. I AM the divine expression of love, manifested in all of creation. As an expression of God, I AM perfect, whole, and complete in every way. I AM perfection everywhere now. I AM perfection here now.

I now therefore claim for myself, [*full name*], my perfect self-expression, led by the Spirit of God, or better, now.

I now know I AM the perfect God-expression, and I freely express my Self with divine grace and dignity, or better, now. I AM free to express my Self in my own unique way. I boldly express my Self the way I AM now, for I AM an expression of God in human form. I allow myself to be my Self without criticism and judgment.

I now release from my mind anything that has prevented my perfect self-expression now, whether known or unknown, conscious or unconscious. I now let go of any and all thoughts and emotions that do not reflect the truth of my being. I now release all thoughts of self-judgment, self-condemnation, self-consciousness, embarrassment, inhibition, awkwardness, shame, shyness, reserve, and reticence now. These thoughts are now lifted, loosed, healed, released, and let go into the light of God's love and truth.

I now accept and welcome new, powerful, positive thoughts and emotions of self-acceptance, self-worth, self-expression, self-love, freedom of expression, extroversion, sociability, unreservedness, conviviality, or better, now.

I now express my Self with strength and courage, knowing I AM worthy to be heard, seen, and appreciated, or better, now. I now know my self-expression is an expression of God, as I AM led by Spirit, now and always. God's guidance leads me to be all I can be, as I express who I really AM, now and forevermore.

I now fully accept, in consciousness, my perfect self-expression, led by the Spirit of God, or better, now. I now thank God for this perfect answered prayer, knowing it does manifest right here and now, under God's grace, in perfect ways. Thank you, God, and SO IT IS.

85. Treatment for Self-Realization

This is a treatment for myself, [*full name*], for my perfect self-realization, or better, now.

I now recognize God is the one truth, one love, one light, the one perfection of being, one and only one—perfect, whole, and complete. God is eternal, uncreated, unborn, undying, without boundaries, unlimited, pure, and whole. God is the source of everything in the universe. God is divine oneness, divine love, divine light, and perfect peace. God is perfection everywhere now. God is perfection here now.

There is nowhere that God is not. God is here, there, and everywhere, within this, that, and everything. Therefore, God is right here, right now, at the very center of my being, within and all around me. I AM one with God, now and always. God's love fills my heart. God's light surrounds me. God's grace sustains me. I AM wholly given to and surrendered to God, which is my fortress, deliverer, redeemer, and sustainer. I AM the divine oneness, love, light, and peace that God is. I AM perfection everywhere now. I AM perfection here now.

I now therefore claim for myself, [*full name*], my perfect self-realization, or better, now.

I now release from my mind any and all negative thoughts, feelings, and beliefs that have prevented me from realizing my true nature of being. I now let go of any and all false beliefs of inadequacy, inferiority, superiority, alienation, lack, unworthiness, confusion, rejection, unforgiveness, anger, resentment, sadness, pain, guilt, shame, procrastination, unkindness, impatience, dependency, and arrogance. These thoughts are now healed, released, blessed, lifted, and let go into the divine light of forgiveness and peace. And they are gone.

I AM now filled with beautiful, powerful, thoughts of truth about myself. I now welcome and accept feelings of adequacy, acceptance, equality, confidence, friendliness, completion, contentment, clarity, love, forgiveness, peace, allowing, happiness, comfort, mercy, kindness, patience, compassion, motivation, independence, and humility. I AM in control of my mind and my life, now and forevermore.

I now know that whatever misconceptions and false beliefs I have accepted and perpetuated about myself are gone. They are lifted into God's love and truth. I now know I AM a divine being of great love, light, peace, power, wisdom, grace, gratitude, forgiveness, and fulfillment. I AM free to be my Self. I AM never anything other than my Self. I AM my true Self, which is perfect, whole, and complete.

I now realize who I really AM, and I express my true Self. I no longer identify with the ego. The small, inadequate vision of self is not who I really AM. I now fully realize and identify with who I really AM—my inner divinity, my true higher Self. I AM that inner divinity. I AM the true Self. I AM the God Self. That I AM, now and always.

I now fully accept, in consciousness, my full and perfect Self-realization, or better, now. I now thank God for manifesting Self-realization now, in my life, under God's grace, in perfect ways. I thank God that this is so now, and SO IT IS.

86. Treatment for Spiritual Enlightenment

This is a treatment for myself, [*full name*], for my perfect spiritual enlightenment, or better, now.

I now recognize there is one power and one presence at work in the universe and in my life: God the good, omnipotent. God is one and only one—one without a second. God is the one truth, the one love, the one light, the one divine intelligence, the one perfection of being. God is good, very good perfection, now. God is perfection everywhere now. God is perfection here now. God is perfect equilibrium, stillness, harmony, equanimity, contentment, serenity, and peace.

I AM now one with, fully merged with, and fully aligned with God in perfect stillness and perfect wholeness. I AM one—one without a second. I AM the one truth, the one love, the one light, the one divine intelligence, the one perfection of being. I AM good, very good perfection now, and eternally sustained. I AM perfection everywhere now. I AM perfection here now. Perfect equilibrium, stillness, harmony, equanimity, contentment, serenity, and peace are within me, at the very center of my being.

I now therefore claim for myself, [*full name*], my perfect spiritual enlightenment, or better, now.

I now release from my mind any and all false beliefs about myself that have blocked or prevented my perfect spiritual enlightenment, or better, now. I now let go of limiting thoughts and emotions that no longer serve me, whether known or unknown, conscious or unconscious. My mind is one with the mind of God in perfect harmony.

I now release all thoughts of illusion, duality, identification, defensiveness, reactivity, lack of discernment, false ego, limitation, bondage, rejection, frustration, anxiety, guilt, blame, mistake, error, foolishness, imbalance, confusion, unworthiness, unkindness, impatience, judgment, coldness, and indifference. And they are gone. They are now burned in the fire of divine love and lifted into divine light.

I now welcome and embrace new, powerful, positive thoughts and emotions. I now accept thoughts of truth, reality, oneness, wholeness, permissiveness, calmness, poise, equilibrium, equanimity, centeredness, self-awareness, self-confidence, determination, purposefulness, meaningfulness, discernment, wisdom, true Self, limitlessness, freedom, acceptance, satisfaction, peace, serenity, tranquility, forgiveness, accuracy, precision, prudence, thoughtfulness, rationality, balance, lucidity, worthiness, kindness, patience, unconditional love, empathy, warmth, compassion, and caring, or better, now.

I now own and express these positive qualities in my life. I now let go of the idea that enlightenment is only meant for great yogis of India. I know enlightenment is for everyone, including me. I now change my life into one of spiritual awakening and enlightenment. I now realize who I really AM. I realize the state of eternal freedom now. I now let go of all seeds of desire that have bound me to the earth plane. I AM free, perfect, complete, and whole. I now know who I really AM—my divine Self, without boundaries, infinite, pure, and whole. I now know I AM That Oneness, you are That Oneness, all this is That Oneness, and That Oneness is all there is.

I now accept fully in consciousness my perfect spiritual enlightenment, or better, now. I now thank God for manifesting this realization in my life now, with God's grace, in God's own wise and perfect ways. I now thank God this is so now, and SO IT IS. SO BE IT!

Part Two
Lifting Your Environment

Chapter 7

Healing Environ-Mental Static

If you are distressed by anything external, the pain is not due to the thing itself, but to your estimate of it; and this you have the power to revoke at any moment.
—Marcus Aelius Aurelius

The world is enveloped by a murky environ-mental cloud, made of the collective thoughts, beliefs, habits, feelings, attitudes, and conditioning of seven billion people. This planetary mental atmosphere has an overpowering emotional and energetic effect, and, to a great degree, determines what people generally accept as truth. Not only does it profoundly influence our beliefs; it is also a barometer, measuring our collective level of consciousness.

Your mental atmosphere surrounds you like the air you breathe. When charged with coherent, positive thought-forms, the emotional climate becomes optimistic, uplifting, and inspirational. When incoherent, negative thought-forms hold sway, then stress and tension rule the day.

Negative or positive emotions are broadcast like radio waves. Every one of your thoughts, words, and deeds radiates from the center of your being into the atmosphere. These waves do not stop at the edge of your body or energy field. They continue to influence the entire universe and then boomerang back to you, exactly as sent.

In this chapter y… ental fallout of environment…

87. H…

Yo… around you through
affirm…

…ness,
To clear, heal, lift, release, and let go
Of all negative thought-forms, emotions,
Beliefs, habits, conditions, and patterns
In the mental atmosphere around me
That have influenced me adversely.
All false, limiting, challenging, difficult.
Overwhelming, draining, and exhausting
Emotions and vibrations in the atmosphere

And in the people and places around me
Are now lovingly blessed, healed, dissolved,
Lifted, released, and completely let go,
Into the light of God's love and truth.
I AM in control of my mind and my life.
I AM the only authority in my life.
I AM divinely protected by the light of my being.
Thank you, God, and SO IT IS.

88. Healing Peer Pressure

Your peers might try to coerce you into sacrificing your own needs in order to fit into a standard set by them. However, your life is your own, and no one else can live it. When you follow your heart, then you remain true to your Self.

I AM in control of my mind and my life.
I AM a being of divine love, light, and truth.
I now let go of any and all seeming need to fit in,
To be normal, to be ordinary, or to act like others.
I now realize there is nothing normal, standard, or ordinary.
I no longer make choices based upon arbitrary ideas
Of normality, abnormality, ordinariness, or extraordinariness.
Though others may put pressure on me
To fit into their mold of what I should be,
I now release, loose, dissolve, and let go
Of any and all need to be someone else's ideal.
I no longer feel the need to impress anyone.
I AM impressive exactly as I AM.
I no longer feel the need to be something I AM not.
I AM perfect exactly as I AM.
I now accept that I AM my Self:
A one-of-a-kind divine original.
I AM unique, perfect, complete, and whole.
Thank you, God, and SO IT IS.

89. Support From Other People

This prayer can help you express your Self as you are, while being supported by peers and loved ones.

In knowing I AM the expression of my divinity,
The divine in divine oneness,

Everyone else supports my progress and my ideals
In the perfect right way, manifesting perfect, right results.
The purity of my intention is manifested in perfection.
Everyone else is supporting my divinity,
As they accept, love, and encourage me
To express my Self as I really AM.
Thank you, God, and SO IT IS.

90. Overcoming False Opinions of Others

This prayer can help you to stay true to your Self and express your perfect divine creativity, talents, and skills, despite the opinions of others.

I AM in control of my life and my mind.
I AM free from the opinions of others.
I AM merged, united, and filled
With the loving, supreme presence of God.
My life is mine, and mine alone.
My mind belongs to me, and me alone.
No one else controls me.
No one has any negative influence upon me.
Whatever others think of me has nothing to do with me.
The opinion of others is no concern of mine.
For no one and nothing can ever shake
My invincible center of being.
I AM powerful, indomitable, impenetrable
Commanding, authoritative, and invincible.
I AM a mighty pillar of strength,
I AM unshakable in my conviction.
My life needs no defense, justification,
Vindication, excuse, or apology.
I AM perfect exactly as I AM. I AM enough.
I AM perfect, complete, and whole.
Thank you, God, and SO IT IS.

91. H

Y ... ur energy field to shrink or be ... d other binding attachments ... ave lasting, devastating effect ... achieving your dreams, then ...

I AM in control of my mind and my life.
My family does not control me.
I AM a radiant being of light,
Filled with God's energy, love, and peace.
I now accept the wisdom learned from my family,
And I cast out all falsehood taught by my family.
I no longer need to try to fit a mold that does not fit.
I create my own mold, based upon divine understanding,
Divine guidance, divine truth, and divine wisdom.
I AM the only authority in my life.
No one and nothing controls me.
My life is guided by Spirit, on the path of wisdom.
I AM on the right path, in the right place,
Doing the perfect right actions for me
With the perfect divine right results.
I AM perfect, exactly as I AM.
Thank you, God, and SO IT IS.

92. Healing Family Karmic Ties

You can heal binding ties with your relatives, both living and dead. If loved ones are tugging on or binding up your mind and energy, use this prayer.

I now know and affirm that my relatives are lifted up
In the cleansing, healing light of God's love.
They now live in a beauteous divine sphere of light,
Protected, whole, and secure in the presence of God.
I know now all my relations are safe, secure, and at peace.
My relatives have no negative effect whatsoever
Upon my God Consciousness now.
All psychic ties, karmic bonds, and binding ties
Between myself and my relations
Are now lovingly cut, cut, cut, cut, cut, cut, cut, cut cut,
Dissolved, released, blessed, healed, let go,
And lifted into the light of God now. And they are gone.
I AM free from all karmic bonds and binding ties.
I AM no longer subject to psychic attacks,
Psychic vampirism, or psychic influence.
I AM free. I AM filled with God's holy presence.
I AM a radiant being of light, filled with God's vibration.

My energy field vibrates and radiates the light of God.
All is perfect and all is well.
Thank you, God, and SO IT IS.

93. Deceased Ancestor Healing

The influence of ancestors does not stop with death. They can affect you adversely, even if you never met them. To heal deceased ancestors that have held you back, use this prayer.

No energy from this world or any other world
Can lessen or diminish my God Consciousness.
All energies from this world and from any other world
That do not reflect the truth of my being
Are now lovingly lifted, healed, blessed, released, let go,
And filled with the light of God.
All seeming influence from past times,
Any and all ancestors that are not in God's light,
And any other dear ones that are here for healing—
All these beings are now lovingly and permanently
Lifted into the light of God's love and truth.
Beloved ones, you are unified with the truth of your being.
You are lifted in love.
God's radiant love, radiant light, and radiant power
Fill and surround you now
With immeasurable peace and immeasurable love.
You are now free from this earthly vibration.
You are free to go into God's holy presence and divine light now.
Go in peace, dear ones, and go in love.
Thank you, God, and SO IT IS.

94. Healing False Societal Beliefs

We are all negatively influenced by the collective beliefs of society around us. Use this prayer to heal the false messages that affect you daily.

I AM in control of my mind and my life.
No one can coerce, manipulate, or dominate me.
I no longer accept any false, mistaken, or deluded
Ideas, concepts, beliefs, conditions, or habits
That anyone or anything has forced upon me.
I no longer trust beliefs, habits, and conditions

That are unreal, untrue, unfounded, and unmerited.
I now dispel all misleading, erroneous, toxic beliefs
That have held me in their grip, whether from
Parents, teachers, friends, counselors, psychics,
Employers, peers, religions, society, Internet, the media,
Or any and all other sources of false ideas,
Whether known or unknown, conscious or unconscious.
I AM now free from false societal beliefs.
I now make decisions based upon inner divine guidance.
I AM no longer bound by society. I AM freed by inner divinity.
I belong to my Self and to God alone.
Thank you, God, and SO IT IS.

95. Healing Brainwashing From Organizations and Cults

If you have been the victim of a coercive organization or cult, use this prayer to free yourself from that influence.

I AM in control of my mind and my life.
Nothing and no one controls me.
I now cut any and all psychic ties, karmic bonds, and binding ties
Between myself and [name of organization and leader].
These psychic ties are all now lovingly
Cut, cut, cut, cut, cut, cut, cut, cut, cut, cut, cut, cut, cut,
Lifted, loved, healed, blessed, released,
And completely let go, into the light of God's love and truth.
I AM in control. I AM the only authority in my life.
I AM divinely protected by the light of my being.
I now close off my aura and body of light to
[Name of organization and leader],
And to anyone and anything but my own inner divinity.
I AM completely free from the influence of
[Name of organization and leader].
I AM free to be my Self. I no longer feel the need
To be a cog in the wheel of [name of organization],
I no longer need to seek approval from anyone.
I no longer need anyone to make decisions for me.
I now make wise decisions based upon
Inner divine guidance and inner knowingness.
I AM free from coercion, manipulation, and intimidation.

105. Healing Massive Groups of Entities

The following prayer can be used to heal massive groups of entities from natural disasters, war zones, and so forth:

I AM one with the light of God.
I now visualize a beauteous golden dome
Of protective divine love and light high above this place.
The Beautiful Many divine beings of light and "I AMs"
Now welcome any and all entities in need of healing now.
These entities are now healed and taken into God's light now.
Beloved ones, you are unified with the truth of your being.
You are lifted in divine love.
You are forgiven of all guilt and shame.
You are healed and released
From loss, pain, confusion, and fear.
Divine love and light fills and surrounds you now.
Attachment to the earth no longer binds you.
You are free to go into the divine light now.
Go now in peace and love.
I now give thanks that part of our assignment on earth
Is to help clear the astral cloud and to pave the way
For the earth's vibrational lifting and enlightenment.
Thank you, God, and SO IT IS.

106. Psychic Vampire Healing Prayer

The legend of vampirism has a corresponding reality in everyday life. Psychic vampires can be either needy people or discarnate entities that tap your energy and suck you dry. Demanding enormous time, attention, love, vitality, resources, and life force, they are bottomless pits into which energy is continually drained. Enabling these people or entities by always saying yes to them never heals them.

Always on the lookout for spigots to hook into, energy suckers see and feel your light, love, and power, and therefore install psychic hooks in your field. Once the pump opens, spiritual energy diminishes from you. Therefore, it is essential to maintain spiritual protection. This prayer, along with the Self-Authority affirmation on page 19, can help.

I AM held in the arms of God. I AM cradled in God's love.
God brings me divine light, radiance, purity, and blessings.
I AM filled with peace, wholeness, and oneness.

Where there is wholeness, there are no parts.
Where there is oneness, there is no psychic vampire,
Psychic drain, psychic sponge, or psychic energy loss.
When there is oneness, there is no loss or gain.
I trust in this oneness and know I AM that oneness.
I AM the true beauteous nature of God beingness.
Thank you, God, and SO IT IS.

107. Psychic Hook Healing

You need not be a victim of psychic vampirism. You can prevent entities from placing hooks in your energy field by using this prayer.

I AM a beloved child of God.
I AM filled with the light of God.
There is no energy that I need fear,
For the Lord my God is with me wherever I go.
There is no energy that has any control over me,
For the Lord my God is with me wherever I go.
There is no entity that can place hooks in me,
For I AM a God-being living in human form and flesh.
I AM a being of great light, of great good,
Of great glory, and of great purity.
God's love fills and surrounds me now.
My heart now melts in divine love.
Thank you, God, and SO IT IS.

108. Healing Reptilians

Reptilian beings, working with demonic energies from the lower astral world, consciously incarnate with malevolent intentions. Their motive is to cause confusion and energy drain, and to confound light workers and spiritual leaders who are lifting the planet. This so-called reptilian energy is a dark astral energy, not extraterrestrial.

Some reptilians have been humans in the past. Others have never been human. These reptilian energies possess enticing and enchanting powers. Certain gurus with reptilian energy build a special mystique and glamour around themselves. Others have a psychic draining or psychic vampire energy.

Use the following prayer if you suspect you are dealing with reptilians.

I now use my power of discernment
To heal and release any seeming reptilian influence now.

I now let go of all fear and transform my energy field,
Through the power of God's love.
All psychic bonds between myself
And seeming reptilian energies
Are now lovingly lifted, healed, untied,
Cut, loved, dissolved, blessed, released,
And completely let go into the light of God now.
There is no longer any influence from reptilian energies now.
Dear seeming reptilian ones,
You are unified with the truth of your being.
You are lifted in divine love. You are filled with the light of God.
You are filled with divine truth. You are filled with forgiveness.
You are free from all contracts and obligations
That you have made with seeming dark forces or energies.
You are free to experience your true nature of being,
And to let go of all fear, glamour, illusion, enchantment,
Charisma, mystique, charm, and ego-enticements.
You are free to be who you truly are.
Open your heart to God's love, God's light, and God's truth.
Let go, let God, and be at peace, dear ones.
Go now into the light of God.
Thank you, God, and SO IT IS.

109. Treatment to Heal Astral Oppression or Possession

This is a treatment for myself, [*full name*], to heal astral oppression or possession, or better, now.

I now recognize God is the one power and one presence in this universe. God is divine strength and invincibility. God is the supreme authority, commanding presence, and just and wise sovereign, ruling with unconditional love. God is the divine healer, which makes all things new and whole. God is perfect oneness and wholeness.

I AM now one with, merged with, and united with God in a perfect seamless wholeness. In God I live, move, and have my being. I AM one with the power, presence, strength, and invincibility of God. I AM one with the supreme authority, commanding presence, just and wise sovereign that God is. I AM one with God's unconditional love and healing power. I AM one with the power that makes all things new and whole. I AM one with perfect oneness and wholeness.

I now therefore claim for myself the perfect healing of astral oppression or possession, or better, now.

I now call upon the Holy Spirit to heal any dear ones that have influenced me or have attached themselves to me. Beloved ones, you are now lovingly healed, lifted, loved, and forgiven. You are unified in love and united with the truth of your being. You are filled, surrounded, and merged with God's love, light, truth, and blessings. This earthly vibration no longer binds you. You are free from fear, pain, confusion, guilt, shame, and loss.

You are bless-ed, forgiven, and released into the love, light, and wholeness of God. You are bless-ed, forgiven, and released into the love, light, and wholeness of God. [*Repeat until it feels complete.*] You are lifted into the light of God, lifted into the light of God. [*Repeat until it feels complete.*] You are free to move into God's light now, into your perfect place of expression. Go now in peace. Go now in love.

I AM now filled, surrounded, and immersed in God's love, God's light, and God's truth. I AM in control. I AM the only authority in my life. I AM divinely protected by the light of my being. My aura and body of light are now closed off to the astral plane, to all astral entities, and to all but my own inner divinity. I now know my energy field is now lifted to the highest possible vibration I can comfortably enjoy. This high-octave energy field now builds a beauteous light-armor made of pure divine love and light.

No force, entity, or energy can invade, take over, oppress, or possess my energy field. I belong to my Self and to God alone. I AM invincible, sovereign, and wholly united with my God Self. I AM a mighty, powerful, spiritual being, filled with the light of God's love. I AM irrepressible, unstoppable, and indomitable. I AM the mighty "I AM" presence, and I AM that inner divinity.

I now fully accept, in consciousness, the perfect healing of astral oppression or possession, or better, now. I now release, loose, and let go of this prayer into the Spiritual Law, knowing it does demonstrate, right here and now, under God's grace, in God's own wise and perfect ways. Thank you, God, and SO BE IT.

110. Treatment for Healing Haunted Buildings

This is a treatment for healing, clearing, and cleansing the seemingly haunted building at [*full address of building*], or better, now.

I now know and recognize God is the only presence and only power at work in the universe. God is the all-loving, all-embracing, all-powerful, all-encompassing sovereign power in the universe. God is the light of life, the truth of being. God is divine love, perfect wisdom, and indomitable strength. God is perfect oneness and wholeness.

I AM now one with God in perfect wholeness and oneness. I AM one with the presence and power of God. I AM one with the all-loving, all-embracing, all-powerful, all-encompassing sovereign power that God is. I AM the light of life, the truth of being. I AM divine love, perfect wisdom, and indomitable strength. I AM perfect oneness and wholeness.

I now therefore know and claim the perfect healing, clearing, and cleansing of the seemingly haunted building at [*full address*], or better, now.

I now know any and all dear ones that have been haunting the building at [*full address*] are now lovingly healed and forgiven, healed and forgiven, healed and forgiven, healed and forgiven. [*Repeat until it feels complete.*] You are bless-ed, forgiven, and released, into the love, light, and wholeness of God. You are bless-ed, forgiven, and released, into the love, light, and wholeness of God. [*Repeat until it feels complete.*] You are lifted into the light of God, lifted into the light of God. [*Repeat until it feels complete.*]

You are unified in love, united with the truth of your being, filled, surrounded, and immersed in the light of God. You are filled, surrounded, and immersed in the love of God. You are now free from guilt, from pain, and from the vibration of the earth. You are now free to go into your perfect divine inner being and your perfect place of expression. Go now in peace. Go now in love.

I now know the building at [*full address*] is now lovingly lifted into the light of God's love. I call upon the Beautiful Many Divine beings who come in the name of God to fill the building at [*full address*] with the light of God. I call upon the Holy Spirit to fill this building with the pure white fire of God. I call forth beautiful Master Jesus to build a beautiful golden sphere of Christ Consciousness light, which permeates and surrounds the entire building. I call upon Archangel Michael to stand above, below, and on every side of this golden sphere, providing divine protection. I call upon Saint Germain to fill this building with the violet consuming, purifying flame of transmutation, which cleanses, heals, and lifts the vibrations in the building. I ask Mahamuni Babaji, the immortal ascended master, to fill this building with the energy of the Himalayas and the siddhas of India. I call forth Mother Mary and Kwan Yin to bring forth the pink light of unconditional love to fill this building with divine love and compassion. This building is now purified with the light of God. It is lifted into a higher octave of vibration.

I now fully accept, in consciousness, that the seemingly haunted building at [*full address*] is now perfect healed, cleared, and cleansed of any seeming haunting, or better, now, and the building is now lifted into a high vibration of divine love. I now thank God for manifesting this perfect healing of the building at [*full address*], or better, now. I now release this prayer into the Spiritual Law of Perfection Everywhere Now, knowing it does manifest right here and now, under grace, in perfect ways. I now thank God that this is so, and SO IT IS.

111. Treatment for Overcoming Psychic Vampirism

This is a treatment for myself, [*full name*], to heal and overcome any and all seeming psychic vampirism in my life, or better, now.

I now recognize God is the one presence and one power at work in the universe and in my life. God is perfect wholeness and oneness. God is the invincible, indestructible presence that governs and sustains the universe. God is the adamantine diamond brilliance that blazes with radiant light. God is perfection everywhere now. God is perfection here now.

I AM one with the presence and power of God. I AM perfect wholeness and oneness. I AM one with the invincible, indestructible presence that governs and sustains the universe. I AM the adamantine diamond brilliance within, which blazes with radiant light. I AM perfection everywhere now. I AM perfection here now.

I now claim for myself the perfect healing and overcoming of any and all seeming psychic vampirism in my life, or better, now.

I now release from my mind, heart, body, and environment any seeming psychic vampirism, or better, now. I now know any and all psychic vampires that have intruded into my life are now lifted into the light of God, lifted into the light of God. [*Repeat until it feels complete.*] They are bless-ed, forgiven, and released into the love, light, and wholeness of God, bless-ed, forgiven, and released into the love, light, and wholeness of God. [*Repeat until it feels complete.*] They are lifted into the light of God's love. And they are gone.

I now call upon the Holy Spirit, the spirit of truth, wholeness, and wisdom, to cut any and all psychic ties between any psychic vampires and me. These ties are now lovingly cut, cut, cut, cut, cut, cut, cut, cut, cut, cut, cut, cut, cut, cut, cut, cut, cut, cut, cut, cut, cut, cut, cut, cut, lifted, loved, healed, released, and let go, into the light of God. I AM now free from any psychic vampires, and they are free from me. I now let go and let God show me the way to a new life, free from codependent relationships and free from energy vampires.

I now know my self-worth and self-respect are no longer dependent upon saving and rescuing other people. I now know that I no longer feel the need to draw into my life weak, needy people who drain my energy, resources, and vitality. I now draw into my life people who support, enrich, inspire, and energize me.

I AM in control of my mind and my life. My true Self is now unconquerable, unshakable, impregnable, unassailable, and invincible. I belong to my Self and to God alone. I AM free from psychic vampirism now.

I now fully accept, in consciousness, my perfect healing and overcoming of any and all seeming psychic vampirism in my life, or better, now. I now thank God for manifesting this perfect healing in my life now, under grace, in perfect ways. I release this prayer into the Spiritual Law, knowing it manifests right here and now. Thank you, wonderful God, and SO IT IS.

Overcoming Enemies and Saboteurs

When there is no enemy within, the enemies outside cannot hurt you.
—African proverb

No matter how much spiritual protection you invoke with prayer, affirmation, and visualization, you might still encounter people who appear to victimize you. They might have designs to control or coerce you against your will. Their methods may include inducing guilt or shame, as they attempt to intimidate or manipulate you for their own selfish ends.

This could manifest as subtle, passive-aggressive behavior; as bossy, overbearing actions; or even as violence. Such domineering people might slander you, file a lawsuit, or try to harm you with black magic. They may attempt to usurp your position at work. They might take credit for your achievements or trample over you to get to the top. They may even try to come between you and your spouse.

Even though, ultimately, you create your own destiny, and you might draw such seemingly abusive situations for a variety of reasons, the reality is that you must find a way to deal with these circumstances. If you feel you are being victimized by any tyrannical person or organization, this chapter can help you heal these relationships.

To learn more about how or why anyone would ever unconsciously create abusive situations in their lives, please read my book *Miracle Prayer.*

112. Psychic Coercion Healing Prayer

When you feel you are being manipulated, coerced, or controlled, or when your self-expression seems to be stifled, you can use this prayer to gain self-authority and break free from a seemingly domineering person or organization.

> *I call upon the Holy Spirit to cut any and all psychic ties*
> *Between myself and* [name of coercive person or organization].
> *These psychic ties are now lovingly*
> *Cut, lifted, loved, healed, released, and let go*
> *Into the light of God's love and truth.*
> *I invoke the divine presence*
> *To eliminate all negations and limitations*
> *That no longer serve me.*

I now dispel all appearances of psychic coercion,
Manipulation, control, and dominance.
And any other thoughts and emotions
That do not reflect the truth of my being.
They are now lovingly lifted, transmuted, and transformed
Through the power of the Holy Spirit.
I AM now open and free to embrace positive,
Life-supporting, energizing thoughts and emotions.
I now welcome thoughts of self-authority,
Self-worth, and freedom of expression.
I call upon Holy Spirit to release all seeming coercion
And to build a beautiful golden sphere
Of protective divine love and light around me.
I call upon Holy Spirit to give me the will
To follow my own true heart and mind now.
I AM in balance. I AM in control.
I AM the only authority in my life.
I AM divinely protected by the light of my being.
I now close off my aura and body of light to
[Name of person or organization],
And to all but my own God Self.
Thank you, God, and SO IT IS.

113. Psychic Implants Healing Prayer

A manipulative, scheming person might deposit implants of psychic ties, bonds, hooks, clamps, plates, and other anomalies into your energy field. These deposits are products of aggression. They can be installed purposefully through energy portals (tubes for traveling into and out of your field), via energy vortices (energy flows going into or out of a portal). You can read more about this in my book *Exploring Auras.* Use the following prayer to heal such anomalies.

Any and all psychic implants, ties, nets, clamps, tendrils,
Tentacles, shackles, cuffs, hooks, plates, and jails
That have been installed in my energy field
Are now evaporated with God's dissolving, purifying acid.
They are now lovingly untied, cut, severed, annihilated,
Healed, released, loosed, blessed, and let go.
Lifted, lifted, lifted, lifted, lifted, lifted, lifted,
Dissolved, dissolved, healed, and released.

They are now burned in God's purifying fire.
I AM now free from all psychic implants now.
They are lifted into the light of God's love.
The source of the implants and their creators
Are now prevented from creating them again.
The beauteous violet consuming flame of Saint Germain
Is now cleansing, clearing, clarifying, purifying,
Healing, lifting, and blessing my energy field.
A tornado of violet fire now moves through my field,
Cleansing, cleansing, cleansing, cleansing,
Healing, healing, healing, healing,
Lifting, lifting, lifting, lifting.
This beauteous, violet, divine flame energy tornado,
Now continues to cleanse my energy field
Until it is no longer needed.
Thank you, God, and SO IT IS.

114. Reversing Black Magic

Black magic is not a myth. It does exist, and there are practitioners of this craft. Some witches use spells for selfish reasons, in order to control others. You might fall under the influence of such psychic manipulation. With this prayer you can heal dark energies, spells, curses, talismans, totems, and black magic.

Any and all astral entities and lower energies
That have been deposited into my energy field
Through totems or talismans, minerals or gems,
Through words, thoughts, psychic vampirism,
Circles, spells, enchantments, curses, black magic,
And all other manipulative methods of psychic coercion,
Whether known or unknown, conscious or subconscious:
These energies are now lovingly healed and forgiven,
Lifted and blessed in divine love, unified with the truth of being,
With God's divine love, divine light, and divine truth.
Beloved ones, go now in love, go now in truth.
You are bless-ed, forgiven, and released
Into the love, light, and wholeness of God's loving presence.
Go in peace now. Go in light. Go in love. Go in peace.
Thank you, God, and SO IT IS.

115. Healing Bullying

To prevent or overcome any seeming intimidation and bullying by tyrants and tormentors, use this prayer, along with the Self-Authority Affirmation on page 19.

I AM in control of my life. I AM not a victim.
I AM a mighty, powerful spiritual being.
I now release, loose, and let go of any thoughts
And emotions that do not reflect the truth of my being.
I now banish all thoughts of weakness, insecurity,
Susceptibility, defenselessness, helplessness,
Self-doubt, anxiety, timidity, and bullying.
And they are gone.
These thoughts are released into the light of God's truth.
I AM now filled with new, powerful, positive thoughts.
I AM invincible, steadfast, strong, powerful, secure, safe,
Confident, invulnerable, assertive, commanding,
Self-assured, poised, outgoing, assertive, and friendly.
I no longer allow anyone or anything to intimidate me.
I AM free from any slings and arrows of bullies.
Nothing can penetrate the impenetrable.
Nothing can violate the inviolable.
I AM that I AM, perfect, whole, and complete.
I stand tall in the truth. I stand in my beingness.
I stand in the unassailable protection of God.
Thank you, God, and SO IT IS.

116. Healing Sabotage

If you are riddled with guilt, shame, and blame, you might draw to yourself experiences of sabotage and subterfuge, which reverse your efforts toward progress in many areas of life. This prayer can help.

God is the all-loving, all-merciful, all-forgiving power,
Which is at work in my life, now and always.
God shines the light of perfect compassion and absolution,
Upon all beings, and upon my life, now and always.
I now release and let go of all seeming guilt and shame
For any seeming wrongdoings I have done
In this lifetime and all past lives.
I now let go of the seeming need to punish myself.
I release all self-sabotage and self-subterfuge.

I now forgive myself completely, for I have always done
The very best I can do in every situation.
I place my life in God's hands,
Knowing that God's unconditional love
Heals and releases me of all seeming wrong and self-blame.
I let go of all addiction to drama and conflict.
I forgive all those who have sabotaged me, including myself.
I know my life is now easy, effortless and joyful,
In divine will and guidance, free from pain, worry, and doubt.
I AM filled with the exquisite beauty that God is.
My life is graced with miracles and wonders.
Thank you, God, and SO IT IS.

117. Divine Justice Healing

When you are dealing with seemingly unjust, unfair, and undeserved situations, where mistreatment, exploitation, and abuse abound, you can use this prayer to help you restore divine justice.

God's divine justice is at work in my life.
God's perfect integrity is within me and all around me.
God's law of justice is working perfectly through me
Toward all people, and through all people toward me now.
I dwell in the circle of divine shelter and protection.
I live in the safe haven of God's abode.
No matter what the circumstance, I AM safe and protected
By the hand of God, which guides me in righteousness.
I walk the perfect right path—the path of truth.
The Law of Justice is at work in my life, manifesting truth.
I AM divinely protected by the light of my being.
Thank you, God, and SO IT IS.

118. Healing and Forgiving Enemies

Forgiveness is a profound healing tool. When you can forgive those who have seemingly wronged you, a great and mighty divine power wells up within you, a power you can use for good.

I now call upon the Holy Spirit,
The Spirit of truth and wholeness,
To shine the light of forgiveness upon me
And upon all seeming enemies in my life.
I now know any apparent enemy is but a reflection

Of my own self-image, seemingly warring against itself.
I now let go of that inner conflict, and I AM at peace.
I now find equanimity, balance, and serenity within.
I know and accept now that because God is for me,
Nothing can ever be against me.
I know and accept now that because I AM one with all,
Nothing can ever be against me,
For I cannot be against my Self.
I now let go of all enmity, conflict, and resentment
Toward anyone and anything that has seemingly
Caused me injury, hurt, damage, or harm.
I cut all psychic ties between myself and all seeming enemies.
These psychic ties are now lovingly cut, cut, cut, cut, cut, cut,
Cut, cut, cut, cut, cut, cut, cut, cut, cut, cut, lifted, loved, healed,
Blessed, lifted, and let go into the light of God's love and truth.
I AM free. I let go and let God be my divine protector.
God is my safe haven of refuge, my sanctuary.
I rush into the precious arms of God, right here and now,
And I AM safe at home with my beloved God.
Thank you, God, and SO IT IS.

119. Divine Shield Prayer

When you know you can call upon divine protection at any moment, there is no reason to be overly concerned about psychic coercion. With God as your anchor, there is nothing to fear. The ultimate truth is that there is no evil "attacking" you. No "bad" energy is "out there." Vampirism is a quality of weakness, and that weakness feeds on those who are similarly weak. As you continue to use affirmations and prayers, such as the Self-Authority Affirmation, you will stay grounded in Spirit, in your true nature of being: God Consciousness. You will no longer unconsciously invite lower energies. This prayer can help.

I AM filled with the light of God.
My cup runneth over.
The light of God fills and surrounds me now.
I AM so full with the divine presence
That nothing else can penetrate my divine beingness.
I AM full. I AM filled with God's strength,
God's power, God's love, and God's light.
I AM complete. I AM whole. I AM one.
Thank you, God, and SO IT IS.

120. Treatment for Overcoming Victimization

This is a treatment for myself, [*full name*], for the complete and perfect overcoming of any and all seeming victimization, or better, now.

I now recognize there is one power and one presence at work in the universe and in my life: God the good, the omnipotent. God is the source of good, the light of life, the perfection of being. God is the rock of power, the pillar of strength, infinitely potent and almighty. God is invincible, unassailable, and immovable. God's energy is boundless, God's life is endless, God's perimeter is limitless, and God's wisdom is matchless. God is perfection everywhere now. God is perfection here now.

I AM now one with, merged with, united with, and aligned with God in a perfect seamless wholeness. God and I are one, in perfect completeness. I AM the light of life, the perfection of being that God is. I AM the rock, the strength, the power, the might that God is. I AM the invincible, unassailable, immovable perfection of being. I AM the boundless, endless, limitless, matchless inner divinity. I AM perfection everywhere now. I AM perfection here now.

I now therefore know and claim for myself, [*full name*], the complete and perfect overcoming of any and all seeming victimization, or better, now.

I now call upon the Holy Spirit to transmute and transform any and all limiting beliefs, habits, and conditions that no longer serve me. I now release all negative thoughts of self-punishment, self-deprecation, self-condemnation, self-hatred, victimization, persecution, unfair treatment, blame, resentment, anger, and rejection. These thoughts are all healed, dissolved, loved, blessed, lifted, released, and let go. And they are gone. They are burned in the fire of God's love and truth.

I now open my heart to God's love, healing, and forgiveness. I accept and welcome into my mind all thoughts of self-forgiveness, self-mercy, self-compassion, pardon, patience, absolution, exoneration, unconditional love, personal responsibility, personal accountability, self-love, self-esteem, self-confidence, and self-empowerment now.

I now know I AM not a victim. Whatever I experience in this life has been magnetized by my own thoughts, words, and deeds, from this life and past lives. I AM responsible for my experiences. Nothing ever happens to me. I only happen to myself. I now forgive myself, and I now bless any person who has seemingly victimized me. For I know that any seeming victimizer was drawn into my life by my own erroneous need for punishment. I now know there is no one to blame for any of my experiences. For all has been created by error-beliefs. I now forgive myself for all past deeds that have caused me to feel a need to be punished. I forgive myself for drawing a victimizer into my life. I love myself, I like myself, I forgive myself, and I accept myself, now.

I now fully accept, in consciousness, that I AM forgiven, and I let go of any and all seeming victimization in my life, or better, now. I now thank God for manifesting this perfect healing in my life, under God's grace, in God's own wise and perfect ways. Thank you, God, and SO IT IS.

121. Treatment for Freedom From Domestic Violence

This is a treatment for myself, [*full name*], for complete freedom from domestic violence, or better, now.

I now know and recognize God is the only presence and only power at work in the universe and in my life. God is the light of life, the truth of being. God is the all that is, the all-loving, all-embracing, all-merciful, all-compassionate, all-powerful perfection of being. God is the sovereign protector, the source of compassion, the perfect safe haven, the comforter. God is divine strength, divine power, divine courage, divine wisdom, and divine discernment.

I AM now one with God—perfect, complete, and whole. In God I live, breathe, move, and have my being. God is within me and all around me. God and I are one. We are in perfect harmony, perfect oneness, and perfect wholeness. I AM the power and presence that God is. I AM the love, mercy, compassion, and perfection that God is. I AM the protector, source of compassion, perfect safe haven, comforter, divine strength, divine power, courage, wisdom, and discernment that God is. I AM all that God is.

I now therefore know and claim for myself, [*full name*], my complete freedom from domestic violence, or better, now.

I AM in control. I AM the only authority in my life. I AM divinely protected by the light of my being. I now close off my aura and body of light to any seeming victimizer, any seeming abuser, and to anyone or anything other than my own inner divinity. I AM in charge of my life. I now cut any and all psychic ties between myself and any seeming abuser. These psychic ties are now lovingly cut, cut, cut, cut, cut, cut, cut, cut, cut, cut, cut, cut, cut, lifted, loved, healed, released, and let go into the light of God's love and truth.

I now let go of all beliefs, habits, patterns, and conditions that have drawn any seeming abuse into my life. I now release all thoughts of abuse, violence, self-deprecation, self-hatred, self-punishment, anger, resentment, blame, guilt, shame, disgrace, unworthiness, lack, frustration, vulnerability, and gullibility. These thoughts are now burned and dissolved in the fire of God's love, and they are gone. I let go of any and all seeming tendency or need for self-punishment or self-abuse. I now forgive myself, for I did the very best I could do in every situation in this life and past lives. Therefore there is no guilt or blame.

I now welcome, accept, and embrace new, powerful, positive thoughts and emotions. I AM filled with thoughts of forgiveness, gentleness, friendliness, peacefulness, self-possession, self-empowerment, self-love, self-worth, self-value, self-esteem, fulfillment, satisfaction, contentment, invincibility, and divine discernment now. I now make wise choices in my life. I choose freedom. I AM free from victimization and abuse, right here and now.

I now walk away from any and all seeming abuse, abusers, victimization, and victimizers in my life. I reach out for help from God, from family, from friends, and from the perfect social and governmental agencies, right here and now. I now accept the proper help, and I walk away right now. I no longer allow or accept any seeming abuse in my life, and I AM free.

I now fully accept, in consciousness, that I AM completely free from any and all seeming domestic abuse, or better, now. I now thank God for manifesting this perfect freedom in my life, under God's grace, in perfect ways. I thank God that this is so now, and SO IT IS.

122. Treatment for Overcoming False Accusations

This is a treatment for myself, [*full name*], to overcome, defeat, and triumph over any and all seeming false accusations that have been unjustly aimed at me, or better, now.

I recognize, right here and now, that there is one power and one presence at work in the universe and in my life: God the good, omnipotent, omnipresent, and omniscient. God is the source of good, the light of life, the truth of being. God is divine justice, with wisdom, impartiality, and righteousness, the perfect arbiter of all seeming conflict. God is honesty and integrity. God is the protector, the comforter, the safe haven.

I AM now one with and merged with God in a perfect seamless wholeness. Wherever I AM, God is. God is within me and all around me. I AM perfectly aligned and united with God. The arbiter of all seeming conflict, filled with divine justice, wisdom, impartiality, and righteousness—that I AM. I AM the protector, the comforter, and safe haven that God is. I AM filled with divine honesty and integrity.

I now therefore know and claim for myself, [*full name*], that I overcome, defeat, and triumph over any and all seeming false accusations that have been unjustly aimed at me, or better, now.

I now know I AM free from any and all psychic slings and arrows that have been seemingly hurled toward me. I now call upon the Holy Spirit to cut any and all psychic ties, karmic bonds, and binding ties between myself and anyone that has wrongly accused me. These psychic ties are now lovingly and completely cut, cut, cut, cut, cut, cut, cut, cut, cut, cut, cut, cut, cut, cut, cut, cut, cut, cut, cut, cut, cut, cut, severed, lifted, loved, healed, blessed, released and let go into the light of God. I AM in control. I AM the only authority in my life. I now close off my aura and body of light to all who have falsely accused me, and to all but my own inner divinity.

I now release from my mind any and all tendency to falsely accuse myself of wrongdoing. I now let go of all thoughts and emotions of guilt, self-deprecation, self-hatred, shame, lack of self-acceptance, and false judgment of self. These limiting thoughts and emotions are gone. They are burned in the fire of God's love.

I AM now open and free to embrace, new, positive, life-affirming thoughts and emotions of self-forgiveness, self-acceptance, self-love, and self-worth. I now realize and know the truth about my Self. I now let go and let God be the arbiter of my life, knowing I AM safe and protected, in God's hands.

I AM now free from any and all seeming false accusations and mudslinging that have been thrown at me. I now know that nothing and no one can shake my invincible connection with God. Nothing and no one can negatively affect my immovable state of well-being. I call upon the Law of Justice to prevail in all situations, and I know divine justice is at work in my life, freeing me from all false accusations now. I know that those who have falsely accused me have no effect whatsoever on my mind or my life in any way.

I now know that whatever I have been falsely accused of now disappears from my life. Any and all plans, schemes, devises, or thoughts of legal action on the part of accusers now vanish in the wind, scattered by the currents of divine love. No legal action can possibly succeed, because no wrongdoing exists. Therefore, I AM free from any and all possibility of negative consequences from false accusations. I AM free, and all seeming false accusations now disappear, harmless and formless, into the universe.

I now fully accept, in consciousness, that I AM free from any and all seeming false accusations directed at me. I now overcome, triumph over, and defeat any and all false accusations, or better, right here and right now. I now thank God for manifesting this divine justice and answered prayer in my life, under God's grace, in perfect ways. Thank you, God. SO BE IT.

123. Treatment for Freedom From Imprisonment

This is a treatment for myself, [*full name*], for my perfect freedom from imprisonment, or better, right now.

I recognize now that God is the one presence and one power at work in the universe. God is perfect divine forgiveness. God is the all-loving, all-merciful, all-compassionate perfection of being. God is divine justice and freedom. God is the safe haven of divine protection.

God's presence and power are at work in my life. I AM the divine forgiveness that God is. I AM the love, mercy, compassion, justice, and freedom that God is. I dwell in the safe haven of protection that God is. God's law of justice is working perfectly through me toward all people, and through all people toward me now.

I now therefore know and claim for myself, [*full name*], my perfect freedom from imprisonment, or better, right now.

I now call upon the Holy Spirit, the spirit of truth and wholeness, to release from my mind any and all thoughts, beliefs, conditions, patterns, and habits that no longer serve me. I now let go of all feelings of guilt, shame, remorse, disgrace, dishonor, humiliation, self-reproach, self-punishment, self-blame, self-incrimination, self-imprisonment, and self-condemnation, and they are gone. They are burned to ashes in the fire of divine forgiveness.

I now know that whatever seeming harm or wrong I have done, in this life or in any previous life, is now wiped clean by the all-loving, all-merciful hand of God. I now know that God, in unconditional love and compassion, forgives me before I even ask. I now know that God pardons all seeming sin and removes all seeming guilt and shame. No matter how despicable and shameful I have felt, I know now that God loves and forgives me unconditionally, right now. God holds me in its loving arms and wipes away all tears.

I now welcome and accept new, beautiful, creative, inspiring beliefs, thoughts, and emotions of forgiveness, pardon, clemency, mercy, absolution, exoneration, self-confidence, self-acceptance, self-respect, self-esteem, dignity, honor, pride, freedom, justice, and gratitude.

I know now that I AM washed clean in the purifying waters of divine love. I bathe in God's loving ocean of forgiveness, and I AM made new. I now know that any seed or tendency toward seeming wrongdoing is removed from my mind, and I AM reborn in the Spirit of God's love. I AM free from any and all criminal activities, and I now turn to God for guidance. I now walk the path of righteousness, and I AM free.

I now accept fully in consciousness that I AM free from any and all seeming imprisonment, or better, right here and now. I now thank God for manifesting my perfect freedom from imprisonment, right now, under grace, in perfect ways. Thank you, God, and SO IT IS.

Making Your Space Into a Cathedral

A person whose mind is free from negative thinking spreads a life-giving influence in much the same way that a tree gives oxygen.
—Eknath Easwaran

Have you ever walked into a building and noticed a dense, low-vibrational feeling that compelled you to immediately run back out? Upon meeting someone, have you ever noticed a strong negative energy that made you want to turn away? If so, then you are sensitive to subtle forces and vibrations.

The majority of your time is spent at home or in the office. Therefore, if those environments have a nurturing, loving, uplifting feeling, then your life will be enhanced. Happily, this feeling is something you can create, even if it does not presently exist.

Two factors are important when considering the energy of any space. First are inherent land energies, such as elevation, mineral deposits, vegetation, animal and bird population, bodies of water, earth vortices, ley lines, and geopathic lines. Second are energies from man-made structures, decor, landscaping, and human thought-forms.

Many people who specialize in creating sacred spaces solely emphasize physical objects and structures, such as altars, meditation rooms, temples, and gardens. However, the higher vibrational energy is not created through physical objects. The lifting of energy arises from an inner expression of love, intention, and divine connection. Because your inner expression is what creates sacred space, the prayers in this chapter can help you transform any space or building into a sacred space.

124. Lifting Any Building or Space

Any space can be lifted with the light, love, energy, peace, grace, and power of God. Just call upon the Holy Spirit to create that higher vibration, and it is done.

I now call forth the Holy Spirit
To lift, heal, cleanse, purify, and sanctify this space.
God is the center of light that fills this space.
God's love permeates and fills this space.
God's light blazes forth and fills this space.
God's peace radiates and fills this space.

God's grace vibrates and fills this space.
This space is now transformed in divine light.
This space is now healed with divine love.
This space is now immersed in divine energy.
This space is now bathed in divine blessedness.
This space is now engulfed in the presence of God.
Thank you, God, and SO IT IS.

125. Blessing a New Home

When you move into a new home, use this blessing to purify negative vibrations and fill the space with pure divine energy. However, this prayer can be used to lift the energy in your home anytime, not just upon moving in.

This home is the house of God.
This home is the temple of God.
This home is the sanctuary of God.
This home is the safe haven of God.
This home is the refuge of God.
This home is immersed in God's love.
This home is radiating with God's light.
This home is blessed with God's grace
In this home, I find comfort.
In this home, I find solace.
In this home, I find wisdom.
In this home, I find joy.
In this home, I find peace.
This home is now blessed
With the beauteous, endless, powerful, healing,
Glowing, joyous, constant stream of God's love.
Thank you, God, and SO IT IS.

126. Lifting the Home Atmosphere

With this prayer, you can transform any home into a heavenly place of love, harmony, peace, and comfort. By calling upon deities and divine beings to fill the home with celestial energies, the energy in that home is lifted to the vibration of God.

This home is now flooded with the light of God.
I call upon the Holy Spirit, the Spirit of truth and wholeness,
To fill this home with divine protection.
I now welcome all the divine beings, ascended masters,

Angels, and archangels, who come in the name of God,
To bless this home with their loving presence.
Please dispel all darkness, and bring forth God's light.
Lift up the vibrational energy in this home
To the highest vibrational octave of energy
That the residents can now comfortably enjoy.
I call upon the Holy Spirit to fill this home
With the white fire of God's peace, love, and harmony.
This entire home is immersed and surrounded
With divine energy, divine light, divine love, and divine grace.
I call upon Master Jesus to build a beauteous golden sphere
Of protective love and light around this home.
I ask this brilliant, dazzling, golden light
To pervade, permeate, and surround this home,
Bringing peace, comfort, security, and divine energy.
I ask Archangel Michael to stand above, below,
And on every side of this shining golden sphere,
Waving his blue flame sword of truth,
Bringing divine protection, security, and safety.
I call upon Saint Germain to fill this home
With the violet consuming flame of transmutation.
This violet fire now whirls throughout this home,
Like a tornado of purifying divine light,
Cleansing, healing, and lifting,
Cleansing, healing, and lifting,
[Continue to repeat until it feels complete.]
Cleansing, healing, and lifting every nook and cranny.
I call forth beautiful Mother Mary and Kwan Yin
To fill this home with the pink light of divine love,
Which brings peace, harmony, strength, and wisdom.
I ask the great Mahamuni Babaji to bless this home
With the clear light of enlightenment, and
To bring forth the energy of the Himalayas,
To saturate this home with the radiant light
Of the immortal Himalayan yogis, rishis, and siddhas.
This home is a temple of the living God,
Bathed in the supernal light of divine love and peace.
Thank you, God, and SO IT IS.

127. Lifting the Workplace Atmosphere (or Places of Business)

By using this prayer, any workplace, company, or organization can become a place of great harmony, peace, cooperation, efficiency, and prosperity. Use this prayer to release negative vibrations and to embrace positive energies.

This workplace is purified, healed, and lifted
By the cleansing action of Saint Germain's violet flame,
Filling every atom of the work environment
With divine love, peace, harmony, and light.
This workplace is richly blessed by the grace of God,
Which brings prosperity, abundance, and wealth,
And which fills the coffers of this enterprise
To its brim and overflowing, or better.
I now release any and all limiting energies
That do not serve this workplace or its workers.
I now release from the mental atmosphere
All false thoughts and beliefs of
Confusion, negligence, carelessness, sloppiness,
Foolishness, dishonesty, deception, subterfuge,
Backbiting, infighting, viciousness, spitefulness,
Impatience, resentment, harshness, retaliation,
Incomprehension, coldness, indifference, intolerance,
Idleness, lethargy, apathy, depression, discouragement,
And all other negative thoughts held in this workplace,
Whether known or unknown, conscious or unconscious.
They are now lovingly lifted, blessed, released, lifted, let go
And dissolved into the light of God's love and truth.
I now claim this workplace is filled
With clarity, focus, precision, accuracy,
Wisdom, integrity, honesty, communication,
Kindness, gentleness, patience, forgiveness,
Understanding, compassion, leniency, tolerance,
Motivation, enthusiasm, inspiration, and joy.
This workplace is a place of God.
God is its employer, God is its employee,
God is its client, God is its vendor,
God is its salesman, God is its customer.
God is in charge of this workplace.

Every person who is encountered at work is God.
I give this workplace over to God, knowing it is
In divine order, divine timing, divine love, divine light,
Divine presence, divine power and divine truth.
Thank you, God, and SO IT IS.

128. Healing Dense Institutional Atmospheres

Old buildings, old institutions, such as schools, colleges, universities, courtrooms, prisons, hospitals, clinics, and mental institutions, are filled with concentrated negative energies and atmospheres. Such dense, tense vibrations feel as if they can be cut with a knife.

I now call forth the Holy Spirit to now lift, heal, and cleanse
This [name of school, college, hospital, prison, institution, etc.],
And to transmute and transform this space
Into a sacred, hallowed, and bless-ed place,
Filled with the brilliant light of God's holy presence.
I now know any and all dear ones
Who have been occupying this space
Are all now lovingly healed and forgiven,
Healed and forgiven, healed and forgiven,
Healed and forgiven, healed and forgiven,
[Continue to repeat until you feel the energy is lifted.]
Lifted in love, united with the truth of your being,
Filled, permeated, and surrounded
With God's love, light, power, presence, and energy.
Free from fear, from pain, and from any and all
Lower, dense, astral vibrational energies,
You are free to move into the divine light now.
Go now in peace and love.
Go to your perfect place of divine expression.
All limiting thought-forms and dense energies in this space
Are now healed, transformed, cleansed, purified, and blessed,
Lifted, lifted, lifted, lifted, lifted, lifted, lifted, lifted,
Into the light of God's love and truth.
This space is transmuted and transformed, lifted and loved.
This space is holy ground. This space is God's home.
This space is God's seat. This space is God's resting place.
This space is God's body. This space is God's presence.

I now call upon the Holy Spirit
To bring forth the energy of divine love right now,
Which fills, permeates, and surrounds this space.
This space is the holy altar of God, right now.
Thank you, God, and SO IT IS.

129. Healing Haunted or Gloomy Buildings

Any haunted building can be healed, transmuted, and transformed into a place of high vibrational energy. No matter how haunted a place is, if the entities inhabiting it are released, and if the space is filled with divine energies, then paradise can be established in that space.

This building belongs to God, and God alone.
This building is no longer occupied
By dense, lower-vibrational energies.
I call upon the Holy Spirit to now bring forth
Any and all dear ones who are here for healing.
These dear ones are now lovingly
Bless-ed, forgiven, and released,
Into the love, light, and wholeness
Of the Universal God Consciousness.
You are lifted in love, filled with God's light,
Free from the density of lower vibrations.
You are lifted into the light of God,
Lifted into the light of God, lifted into the light of God,
[Repeat until you feel the lifting of consciousness.]
Living in the light of God, living in the light of God,
[Repeat until you feel complete.]
Free to express your true nature of being.
Free to be your divine Self, who you truly are.
Go now, in peace and love, into the divine light.
I now know that God's holy presence
Now fills, pervades, and surrounds this building,
Bringing forth divine energy, love, light, and peace.
This building is now transformed into a sacred space,
Filled with the light of God's love.
Thank you, God, and SO IT IS.

130. Healing Churches, Temples, Synagogues, or Sacred Spaces

Most people imagine religious buildings would be filled with uplifting, divine energies. However, the reality is most of these buildings are crowded with negative thought-forms, dense energies, astral entities, and a sad, depressing atmosphere. Unfortunately, the average clergyperson is not sensitive to these negative energies, and is clueless about how to heal and lift the atmosphere in his or her building.

This [name of church, temple, synagogue, worship place, sacred space]
Is now filled with the light of God's love and truth.
Any and all limiting, negative, dense vibrations
That have been attached to this space,
Are now lovingly lifted into the presence of God.
They are now healed and forgiven,
Lifted in love, united with the truth of being.
Filled, surrounded, and healed in God's love,
Filled, surrounded, and healed in God's light.
Free from fear, from pain, and from the earthly vibration,
Free to go into the light of God. Go now in peace.
You are now free. You are now home again. You are beloved.
I now call upon the Holy Spirit to
Purify, heal, and cleanse this space
In the crystal clear, stainless, pure waters
Of God's holy, divine presence.
This space in which I stand is holy ground.
This space is now charged, energized, filled,
Permeated, pervaded, and surrounded
With the pure white light of God.
This space is lifted to the highest possible vibration
That is comfortable and inspiring for all those who visit.
This space is the altar of God. This space is God's home.
This space is God's dwelling place, now and always.
Thank you, God, and SO IT IS.

131. Prayer of Unification for Groups

This prayer is used to unify and lift the atmosphere of a group doing spiritual work, such as a workshop, group meditation, healing group, prayer circle, or other spiritual gathering.

We are now one with each other.
We are one with God.
We are one with the truth of being.
We are one with the light of God Consciousness.
We are one with the infinite divine intelligence.
We are one with the perfection of being.
We are one with perfection everywhere now.
We are one with perfection here now.
We are one with the indwelling Spirit of God.
We are one with God's love, one with God's light,
One with God's energy, and one with God's truth.
We are now one in Spirit.
Thank you, God, and SO IT IS.

132. Treatment to Lift Atmospheres and Spaces

This is a treatment for the perfect lifting of the vibrational energy of this space into the vibration of perfect divine energy, or better, now.

I now recognize that God is the one presence and one power at work in the universe. God is perfect wholeness and oneness. God is the omnipresent energy that pervades all space, all time, and all things. God is everywhere present—here, there, and everywhere, within this, that, and everything. God is perfect divine spiritual energy, perfect absolute bliss consciousness, perfect peace, perfect contentment, perfect serenity, perfect harmony, perfect joy, perfect equanimity, perfect light, perfect love, perfect truth. God is perfection everywhere now. God is perfection here now.

I AM now one with, merged with, aligned with, and united with God, in a perfect seamless wholeness. In God I live, breathe, move, and have my being. God is within me and all around me, within every particle of my being. I AM the omnipresent energy that God is. I AM the perfect divine spiritual energy, perfect absolute bliss consciousness, perfect peace, perfect contentment, perfect serenity, perfect harmony, perfect joy, perfect equanimity, perfect light, perfect love, and perfect truth that God is. I AM perfection everywhere now. I AM perfection here now.

I now therefore know and claim the perfect lifting of the vibrational energy of this space into the vibration of perfect divine energy, or better, now.

I now know this space is filled with God's loving energy. Any and all dear ones who are here for healing are now lovingly healed and forgiven, healed and forgiven [*repeat until it feels complete*], unified with the truth of your being, filled with the radiance that God is, filled with the love that God is. You are free from fear, from pain, free from the astral plane and free from the earth plane.

You are bless-ed, forgiven, and released, into the love, light, and wholeness of God Consciousness. You are bless-ed, forgiven, and released, into the love, light, and wholeness of God Consciousness. [*Repeat until it feels complete.*] You are free to move into the divine light now. You are lifted into the light of God, lifted into the light of God. [*Repeat until it feels complete.*] Go into the divine light now. Go now in peace and love.

I now know this space is purified, cleansed, healed, and transformed by the blazing violet consuming flame of Saint Germain. That violet fire of transmutation is whirling, swirling, and dancing through this space, filling, surrounding, permeating, and pervading this entire space—lifting, healing, cleansing, purifying, and releasing all dark energies, lifting them into the light of God, and filling this space with the radiance of God's light.

The vibration of this space is now lifted, blessed and healed, lifted, blessed and healed [*repeat until it feels complete*], lifted into the light of God's love and truth. I now call forth Saint Germain to lift this space into a higher octave of vibration, to the vibration of God Consciousness, or better. This space is now healed, cleansed, and lifted to the highest octave of vibration possible that can be comfortably enjoyed at this time.

I now call forth all the divine beings of light, aspects of my higher Self, deities, angels, and archangels, and deities who come in the name of God. I ask these beauteous beings of light to fill this space with their luminous vibration, and to encircle this space, lifting its energy into God's light, bringing divine protection and divine love. This place on which I stand is holy ground. This place is God's dwelling place. It is sacred, holy, and blessed. It is the house of the Lord. It is the safe haven of God. This is place is filled, surrounded, and pervaded by God's holy presence. I now open my heart of God's love, and I AM at peace in this place of perfect peace. This space is the altar of God, and I now open to receive its blessings.

I now accept fully, in consciousness, the perfect lifting of the vibrational energy of this space into the vibration of perfect divine energy, or better, now. I now thank God for manifesting this perfect good in my life, under God's grace, in God's own wise and perfect ways. I now release this prayer into the Spiritual Law of Perfection Everywhere Now. Thank you, God, and SO IT IS.

Part Three

Making Dreams Come True

Living in Perfect Health

But they that wait upon the Lord shall renew their strength; they shall mount up with wings as eagles; they shall run, and not be weary; and they shall walk, and not faint.
—Isaiah 40:31

While you are in good health, you can easily make spiritual progress. Meditation, prayer, and spiritual practices are possible only when your attention is not preoccupied with health problems. If health is compromised, then every effort, in both the material and spiritual realms, becomes a challenge. Therefore, preserving your health, the precious gift of God, is your utmost priority.

There are five main spokes on the wheel of perfect health—physical, mental, emotional, spiritual, and material. When you maintain your center at the axis of this wheel, you allow the wheel of health to roll smoothly along life's pathway. By developing and retaining good health in all five domains, you sustain your life in balance. This chapter can help you develop and maintain good spiritual, emotional, mental, physical, and material health.

133. Perfect Physical Health

By affirming perfect physical health and vitality, you can create it. Ask, and you will receive.

I now call upon the Holy Spirit,
The spirit of wholeness,
To bring forth into my body
Perfect, robust health and well-being.
I AM filled with pranic life force energy,
Which courses through my body,
Energizing and lifting my energy field,
And filling me with perfect health.
My body is strong, powerful, and healthy right now.
I AM in perfect physical health.
Thank you, God, and SO IT IS.

134. Perfect Mental Health

Mental health is even more important than physical health, because the cause behind the cause of all illness, dis-ease, and dis-comfort is mental in origin.

My mind is saturated and immersed
In the light and presence of God.
I now dissolve, release, loose, and let go
Of any and all limiting thoughts and feelings
That no longer serve me.
I now release all thoughts of anger, resistance, confusion,
Anxiety, fear, frustration, guilt, blame, unworthiness,
Sadness, pain, lack, limitation, incompleteness, illness,
And any other error-thoughts in my mind.
I now welcome into my mind powerful, positive, pure
Thoughts and feelings that enhance my life.
I AM filled with thoughts of peace, acceptance, clarity,
Relaxation, courage, strength, satisfaction, forgiveness,
Letting go, self-worth, happiness, joy, ease, comfort,
Limitlessness, completeness, contentment, love, and health.
I AM in control. I AM the only authority in my life.
I AM divinely protected by the light of my being.
My mind is now fully aligned with the mind of God.
I AM now in perfect mental health.
Thank you, God, and SO IT IS.

135. Perfect Emotional Health

Your emotional state of health determines both your physical and mental well-being. When emotions are in equanimity, then your life is smooth, comfortable, and at ease.

God is my center and circumference of well-being.
My emotions are now stable and balanced.
I AM filled and surrounded by an ocean of tranquility.
I stand in the light of God, immersed in divine serenity.
I stand firm in balance, moderation, equanimity,
Equilibrium, relaxation, quietude, and stillness.
No one and nothing can shake me
From my rock solid, perfectly still, center of being.
God's love directs and controls my emotions.
God's light shines the truth upon my emotions.
I AM invincible in the presence of God's love.
I AM at peace, surrounded by the light of God.
I AM now in perfect emotional health.
Thank you, God, and SO IT IS.

136. Perfect Spiritual Health

Spiritual health is the foundation an 1 the presence of God, your spiritual healtl

With God, I AM whole.
With God, I AM complete.
With God, I AM my Self.
With God, I stand in the perfection of being.
With God, I live my true purpose and destiny.
With God, I dwell in safety and security.
With God, I walk in grace and blessedness.
With God, I AM content.
With God, I AM at home.
With God, I AM at peace.
I AM in perfect spiritual health, right here and now.
Thank you, God, and SO IT IS.

137. Perfect Material Health

Aligning yourself with God's love, light, presence, wisdom, and guidance brings well-being, ease, comfort, content, grace, and blessings in material life.

My life is filled with the light of God.
My life is maintained by the presence of God.
My life is guided by the wisdom of God.
My life is saturated with the love of God.
I AM living my true purpose and divine plan,
Which brings me happiness, content, and joy.
I AM divinely guided and inspired,
Which fills me with confidence and direction.
My life is blessed with wonders and miracles,
For I AM attuned to the divine presence,
Which is my source of supply and bringer of plenty.
I claim my good, very good perfection now,
And eternally sustained.
I AM now in perfect material health.
Thank you, God, and SO IT IS.

138. Divine Idea of Health

Perfect wellness is the perfect idea in the mind of God, made manifest by demonstrating that idea in your body. Health is the truth, and anything unlike health is false.

I AM a child of God; therefore, I inherit only perfect health.
I AM one with the radiant living substance of God;
Therefore I AM hearty, whole, and well.
Let the light of God's love, life, and healing power in me
Burst forth with the brilliance of glowing health, right now.
I AM full of life—healthy, wholesome, vigorous,
Sound, whole, and complete in every area
Of my body, mind, emotions, spirit, and life.
My body is the substance of God,
Manifesting in correspondence with God's perfect idea.
My health is a result of my belief
In the divine idea of God's pure life.
Therefore, I AM in perfect health.
Thank you, God, and SO IT IS.

139. Restoring Perfect Health

God has created this perfect body as a self-correcting, self-healing mechanism. Illness is created by the mind, which mistakenly sees duality rather than perfect unity. The truth is that the body can be and is now restored to perfect health.

I AM one with the presence of God.
God's restoring and renewing power
Is at work in my life, returning me to perfect health.
My body is perfect. My health is perfect.
Divine energy flows freely through my body,
Bringing unlimited life force energy and vitality.
I AM robust, healthy, vigorous, and hearty.
I AM filled with enormous strength and fitness.
I AM filled with wellness, stamina, and power.
I AM filled with energy, dynamism, and wholeness.
Thank you, God, and SO IT IS.

140. Body of God Prayer

When you see yourself as God, you see the truth. God is everywhere present—here, there, and everywhere, in this, that, and everything. Therefore, God is here within you, also. As a divine being, you are in all ways perfect.

I AM created in the likeness and image of God.
My body is the body of God.

Therefore, I have the DNA of God.
My body looks like God, feels like God, acts like God,
And responds like God to all seeming challenges.
God's life-giving pranic energy and perfect health
Flow through every atom, molecule, and cell.
Thank you, God, and SO IT IS.

141. Perfect Diet

Because your body is a sacred vessel, treat it with respect by feeding it nutritious, life-giving foods.

My body is the temple of God.
Therefore I treat this sacred vessel with honor and respect.
I no longer ingest life-damaging foods, devoid of nutrition.
I now intake only nutritious, life-giving foods.
My inner divinity is perfect, complete, and whole,
And my diet is a perfect reflection of my inner divinity.
At the grocery story and the restaurant,
I make wise and purposeful decisions.
God supports me in building constructive, healthy habits.
I choose life.
Thank you, God, and SO IT IS.

142. Grace Before Meals

This prayer can be recited before meals to invoke beauteous qualities of God that imbue the food with life-giving, life-nourishing, and life-sustaining qualities.

This food is the bounty of God, which fills me.
This food is the gift of God, which comforts me.
This food is the grace of God, which heals me.
This food is power of God, which strengthens me.
This food is the joy of God, which satisfies me.
This food is the love of God, which nourishes me.
This food is the energy of God, which invigorates me.
I now eat this food with respect and reverence,
Knowing God's boundless energy is in every mouthful.
God now sustains perfect health through me,
As this food is now consecrated with God's grace.
I now dine at God's table and I receive God's blessings.
Thank you, God, and SO IT IS.

143. Perfect Exercise

Body movement, stretching, and moderate exercise enhance health and well-being. Yet bodily exhaustion through over-exertion or through damaging drugs is deleterious to health and to peace of mind.

God's presence manifests perfectly in this body
As perfect divine energy and robust health.
I therefore treat this body as a temple of God.
I now bring vigor, rejuvenation, and strength to this body
Through movement, stretching, and exercising.
I enjoy the feeling in this body
Of greater flexibility, flow, grace, energy, and well-being
That results from the perfect daily exercise
That is proper for my body size, shape, and weight.
I now stay healthy, strong, and vital throughout my life.
I maintain and enhance my robust, vital health now.
I AM in perfect health, now and always.
Thank you, God, and SO IT IS.

144. Ease and Flexibility

When you imbibe divine grace, your body, mind, and life are filled with ease, comfort, and flexibility.

I AM flexible, agile, and flowing.
I AM graceful in all I do.
I AM divinely coordinated.
I always move smoothly and elegantly,
With divine grace and effortlessness.
I move forward in life with simplicity,
I relax and let life flow through me with ease.
I gently move through each new experience.
I AM at peace with where I AM.
I let go of all expectations.
Joy delights me at every turn.
All is well.
Thank you, God, and SO IT IS.

145. Ideal Body Size, Shape, and Weight

Everyone has an ideal body size, shape, and weight for maximum health. Starving yourself to emaciation or stuffing yourself to obesity is not conducive to health and well-being.

This body is the body of God, and I treat it as a sacred vessel.
I AM now free from any and all seeming need
To be overweight or underweight.
Whatever error-beliefs have motivated me
To stuff my body with excess food,
Or to starve myself in order to be underweight,
Whether known or unknown, conscious or unconscious,
Are now lifted, healed, released, and let go now.
I now allow my body to attain perfect balance.
My body now maintains the ideal size, shape, and weight
For my optimum perfect health.
Thank you, God, and SO IT IS.

146. Letting Go of Body Padding

Some people have unconsciously padded their bodies in an effort to protect themselves from negative energies. By using this prayer, along with the Self-Authority Affirmation on page 19, they can overcome the tendency to cushion the body in this way.

This body is perfect, complete, and whole, as God is.
I now let go of any and all seeming need
To pad my body or create a cushion to protect myself.
I no longer feel any seeming need
To make myself invisible or to block love from my life.
I no longer feel any seeming need
To numb myself from low vibrations around me.
I no longer feel any seeming need
To block myself from energies that drain me.
I no longer feel any seeming need
To stop the pain of feeling negative emotions.
I no longer feel any seeming need
To stuff down emotions through stuffing myself with food.
I now release, shed, and let go of excess weight from my body.
I now know I AM safe and secure in the arms of God.
I now welcome and accept love into my life.
I now embrace all kinds of emotions.
I AM perfect and whole, in every way, exactly as I AM.
Thank you, God, and SO IT IS.

147. Healing a Body Part

Use this healing prayer to restore, renew, and repair a limb, organ, system, or other body part. Your body can be made whole again.

My body rests in the hands of God.
God, the renewing power and divine medic,
Heals and restores my body to perfect health.
My [name of body part here] *is now healed of all seeming*
Dis-ease, dis-comfort, pain, illness, and disorder,
Through the power and presence of the Holy Spirit.
I AM restored, whole, and well, and in perfect health now.
I AM restored, whole, and well, and in perfect health now.
[Repeat until you feel a positive shift in energy.]
I AM the resurrection and the life.
I AM the resurrection and the life.
[Repeat until you feel a positive shift in energy.]
Thank you, God, and SO IT IS.

148. Healing of Eyesight or Hearing

When some people have traumatic experiences, their eyes and ears are weakened. Others lose eyesight and hearing as they age. This prayer can help restore your precious senses of sight and sound.

I AM lifted up into the light of God.
I AM moved by God's glorious presence.
I see only beauty and I hear only good,
Even in the seeming appearance of evil.
I now let go of all traumatic sights and sounds,
And I see the world through the eyes of God.
I hear the tender voice of God's message.
I feel the blessings of God's grace.
My eyes see the glory of God.
My ears hear the music of the spheres.
I AM healed of all seeming diminishment
Of eyesight or hearing now.
My eyes and ears are in perfect health.
Thank you, God, and SO IT IS.

149. God's Living Substance

God's living substance and the divine idea of pure life and energy refreshes and renews the body with health, energy, well-being, and harmony.

I AM one with the radiant, living substance of God.
The light of God's love, life, and healing power in me
Now bursts forth with the brilliance of glowing health.
My body is the substance of God,
Manifesting in correspondence with God's pure life.
The life of God is released in me,
And I AM alive with vibrant energy.
As I think positive, health-enhancing thoughts,
My mind and body are restored to perfect balance.
The life of God within me
Now returns me to harmony, strength, and health.
I AM renewed. I AM rejuvenated. I AM healed.
Thank you, God, and SO IT IS.

150. God's Mighty Healing Current

The mighty healing current of God, which is the revitalizing power in the breath, floods the body with health and well-being.

My body is the shrine of God,
Therefore God is present in every cell.
"Yes" is the response of my cells to words of life and healing.
Every cell is quickened with joy and nourished with love.
God-life flows through my body
As a mighty current of cleansing and healing.
God's vitalizing energy floods my entire being.
I AM immersed in the presence of God.
I AM restored in mind, body, and soul.
I AM a new creation,
Energized by the healing, revitalizing power of God.
Every breath I take refreshes and renews me.
I AM healed. I AM whole.
Thank you, God, and SO IT IS.

151. Prayer Treatment for Healing a Disease

This is a treatment for myself, [*full name*], for the perfect healing of any seeming appearance of [*insert name of disease here*], or better, now.

I now recognize there is only one healing power and one healing presence at work in the universe and in my life: God the good, omnipotent. God is the divine physician, the bless-ed restorer and renewer of health and well-being. God is the source of life force energy, the creator of all life in the universe. God breathes life into all beings and sustains life in all beings. God is the divine healer. God is perfection everywhere now and in all things. God is perfection here now and in myself.

I AM now one with, merged with, fully aligned with, fully united with, fully sustained by, and fully restored by the power and the presence of God. In God I live and move and have my being. I AM the divine physician and healer that God is. I AM the restorer and renewer that God is. I AM the sustainer and life-giving power that God is. The healing power and presence of God is within me, at the center of my being. I AM perfection everywhere now. I AM perfection here now.

I now therefore claim for myself, [*full name*], the perfect healing of any seeming appearance of [*insert name of disease here*], or better, now.

I now release, dissolve, and let go of any and all seeming appearance of [*name of disease*], or better, now. This seeming [*name of disease*] is now lifted, loved, healed, blessed, dissolved, released, let go, and burned to ashes in the fire of God's perfect love.

Whatever the cause behind the cause behind the cause of this seeming appearance of [*name of disease*], whether conscious or unconscious, known or unknown—that seeming cause and any error-thinking behind that cause are now lovingly lifted, healed, dissolved, released, and let go, into the light of God's love and truth. And they are gone. My mind is one with, attuned with, and united with the mind of God. I AM filled with the presence of God.

I release from my mind now all thoughts, feelings, and emotions that no longer serve me. I release, loose, and let go of any and all thoughts of anger, resentment, fear, remorse, regret, guilt, shame, self-punishment, self-pity, illness, disease, discomfort, pain, sadness, depression, doubt, unworthiness, frustration, anxiety, confusion, and suffering. These error-thoughts are now healed and lifted into the light of God. And they are gone. They are burned and dissolved in the fire of God's love and mercy.

I now open my heart to receive new, positive, powerful truth-thoughts of peace, forgiveness, self-acceptance, self-worth, self-love, adequacy, faith, trust, courage, strength, personal responsibility, praise, wellness, well-being, vitality, heartiness, vigor, life force energy, perfect health, comfort, happiness, joy, upliftment, inspiration, contentment, tranquility, clarity, and wholeness. I welcome these thoughts now, and I AM healed.

I AM in control of my mind now and always. I now release any seeming appearance of [*name of disease*] now, and it is lifted into the light of God, lifted into the light of God [*repeat until if feels complete*], and it is released, formless and harmless, into the universe. It is gone.

I now fully accept, in consciousness, my perfect, perfect healing of any seeming appearance of [*name of disease*], or better, now. I now release and let go of this prayer treatment into the Spiritual Law, knowing it is accepted now, and it is done as stated, or better, now. Thank you, God, and SO IT IS.

152. Treatment for Healing Cancer

This is a treatment for myself, [*full name*], for my perfect, complete healing of any seeming appearance of cancer, or better, now.

I now recognize God, the source of all life, is the one healing power and one healing presence at work in the universe. God is the miracle-making power. God is the reservoir of cosmic energy. God is the source of health, the consummate healer. God is perfect well-being and divine vitality. God is the divine physician, the renewer of health and restorer of strength. God's love makes all things new, throughout the cosmos.

I AM now perfectly united and aligned with the source of all life that God is, the one healing power and presence at work in the universe. I AM now one with the reservoir of cosmic energy, the miracle-making power that God is. I AM now one with the source of health, the consummate healer. I AM one with perfect well-being and divine vitality. I AM fully merged with the divine physician, the renewer of health and restorer of strength. God's love makes all things new, for and through me.

I now therefore claim for myself, [*full name*], my perfect, complete healing of any seeming appearance of cancer, or better, now.

I now release, loose, and let go of the cause behind the cause of any seeming appearance of cancer now. Whatever thoughts and emotions have caused cancer to seemingly appear in this body are now lovingly lifted, healed, released, dissolved, and let go into the light of divinity now, and they are gone.

I now dispel from my mind any and all thoughts of anger, resentment, frustration, anxiety, stress, pressure, limitation, worry, doubt, fear, guilt, blame, shame, unworthiness, self-destruction, self-punishment, self-annihilation, and death-wish now. These thoughts are now lovingly blessed, lifted, loved, healed, released, and let go. And they are gone. They are now burned in God's loving, all-consuming fire of transmutation.

I now welcome and embrace new, beautiful, life-enhancing, fulfilling, radiant thoughts and emotions of love, peace, forgiveness, happiness, patience, calm, balance, equilibrium, equanimity, limitlessness, faith, trust, certainty, wisdom, self-love, self-worth, self-esteem, self-forgiveness, self-empowerment, self-responsibility, self-actualization, gratitude, and life. I welcome and embrace life into my life now.

I AM in control. I AM the only authority in my life. I AM divinely protected by the light of my being. I now close off my aura and body of light to all seeming appearance of cancer, and to all but my own inner divinity.

I now know any and all untoward energies that have seemingly attacked my body and caused the cause behind the cause of the seeming appearance of cancer are now lovingly healed and forgiven, lifted in love, unified with the truth of being, filled with the radiant light of God, surrounded by the loving presence of God, free from fear, free from pain, free from the material vibration, free to move into the light of God. These energies are now bless-ed, forgiven and released into the love, light, and wholeness of God. They are lifted into the light of God. Go now in peace and love.

I now welcome and embrace God's healing balm, which fills my mind and body with renewed strength and vigor. I now bathe in the healing ocean of God's liquid love, which fills and surrounds me with perfect oneness. I now open to the healing light of God's radiance, which streams into my being with divine energy. I now receive God's infinite, perfect blessings and grace, which now fill, surround, penetrate, permeate, and engulf my body, bringing health and wellness right now. I AM now fully immersed in God's mighty healing power, which restores my body to perfect health right now. I AM now renewed and invigorated by the power and presence of God.

I now fully accept, in consciousness, my perfect, complete healing of any seeming appearance of cancer, or better, now. I now give gratitude to God for my perfect, complete, permanent healing of the seeming appearance of cancer now, under God's grace, in perfect ways. I now release this prayer into the Spiritual Law, knowing it does manifest right here and now, under divine grace, in perfect ways. Thank you, God, and SO IT IS.

153. Treatment for Healing Heart Disease

This is a treatment for myself, [*full name*], for my perfect, complete permanent healing of any seeming heart disease, or better, now.

I now know and recognize God is the creator of all living things in the universe. God is life force energy. God gives life to all things, now and always. God is perfection everywhere now. Therefore, God's creation is perfect in every way. God creates perfection in every being, with perfect, self-correcting, self-healing bodies. God is the divine medic, the ideal, supreme healer.

I AM now merged, united, and one with God. My body is the temple of God. Therefore, God is present in every cell. I AM created in the likeness and image of God. Therefore, I have the DNA of God. My body looks like God, feels like God, and responds like God to all seeming dis-ease. God's life-giving energy flows through every atom, molecule, and cell of my body.

I now therefore claim for myself, [*full name*], my perfect, complete permanent healing of seeming heart disease, or better, now.

I now know my body is healed of all seeming dis-ease now. I now allow God's perfect self-correcting mechanism to heal my body and to restore the wholeness and oneness of perfect health. I know the perfect, life-giving pranic energies are now flowing through my subtle body freely, without resistance. My entire circulatory system is functioning perfectly.

I now release from my mind any and all thoughts and emotions—known or unknown, conscious or unconscious—that have contributed to seeming heart disease within my body. My mind is now one with and aligned with God's mind. I now let go of all negative thoughts of guilt, strain, anxiety, stress, hypertension, pressure, fear, pain, contraction, constriction, sadness, isolation, and loneliness. These thoughts are all now lovingly healed, blessed, lifted, released, and let go, into the light of God's love and truth.

I now welcome, accept, and embrace powerful, positive, beautiful, optimistic, new, creative thoughts of forgiveness, relaxation, peace, calm, serenity, tranquility, health, divine circulation, lightness, love, ease, comfort, effortlessness, expansion, joy, happiness, friendship, and love.

I AM in control of my mind and my life. I now welcome an effortless, easy life of comfort, guided by Spirit, with love all around me. I now allow my heart to open to loved ones and friends around me. I AM filled with God's loving energy, and I AM healed.

I now fully accept, in consciousness, my perfect, complete, permanent healing of seeming heart disease, or better, now. I now give gratitude to God for this healing, knowing it does demonstrate perfectly right now, with divine order and timing. Thank you, God, and SO IT IS.

154. Treatment for Healing Injuries

This is a treatment for myself, [*full name*], for perfect healing of any and all seeming injury of [*insert description of injury here*], or better, now.

I recognize that there is but one life. That life is God. There is but one mind and one power, which is God. God is life that heals all, wisdom that guides all, and love that comforts all. God is the one healing power and one healing presence in the universe. God is the divine physician, the celestial medic, the source of health, the consummate healer. God is the reservoir of cosmic energy. God is perfect well-being and divine vitality.

There is nowhere that God is not. God is within me and all around me. I AM one with the life that is God. I AM one with the healing power, healing presence, and wisdom that God is. I AM unified with the divine physician, celestial medic, and consummate healer, which is God. I AM one with God's reservoir of cosmic energy, well-being, and vitality. I open my heart to the sacred presence of God, and I trust in God's enduring love.

I now therefore claim for myself the perfect healing of any and all seeming injury of [*description of injury*], or better, now.

I now know God's miracle-making power now heals any and all seeming wounds and injuries in my body, quickly, beautifully, perfectly, with divine order and timing, right here and now. All seeming wounds and injuries are now divinely protected, free from any seeming infection or contamination, right now. My body heals seamlessly, without scar or disfiguration, right now.

My body is renewed and perfectly restored by the healing power of God. It is made whole and new with God's perfect healing power. I now accept fully in consciousness, the perfect healing of any and all seeming injury of [*description of injury*], or better, now. I now thank God for manifesting this perfect healing and complete restoration of perfect health in my life, under grace, in perfect ways. I now release this prayer into the Spiritual Law, knowing this healing takes place right now, under grace, in perfect ways. Thank you, God, and SO IT IS.

155. Treatment for Recovery From Surgery

This is a treatment for myself, [*full name*], for perfect recovery from surgery, or better, now.

I now recognize God is the mighty pillar of strength and power. God is the all-powerful, everlasting, perpetual, ceaseless source and continual flow of divine vitality, energy, restoration, and renewal. God has no boundaries or limitations. God is the miracle-making power, which makes all things new and whole. God is life force energy. God is perfection everywhere now.

I AM now one with the mighty pillar of strength and power that is God. I AM the all-powerful, everlasting, perpetual, ceaseless source and continual flow of divine vitality, energy, restoration, and renewal. I AM without boundaries or limitations. The miracle-making power, which makes all things new and whole, is at work in my life, renewing and restoring my body to wholeness. I AM one with God's life force energy. I AM perfection everywhere now.

I now therefore claim for myself, [*full name*], perfect recovery from surgery, or better, now.

I know my body is restored to robust health right now. I now let go of any and all thoughts and emotions that no longer serve me. I release from my mind all thoughts of illness, disease, ill-health, weakness, sickness, frailty, feebleness, debility, infirmity, and any other thoughts and emotions that have affected me adversely. These thoughts are now lifted, healed, blessed, released, and let go into the light of God.

I AM now filled with thoughts of perfect vitality, health, happiness, joy, wellness, strength, power, force, well-being, vigor, robustness, and life force energy. I AM in control. I AM the only authority in my life. I AM divinely protected by the light of my being. I AM now filled with vital pranic energies, flowing freely and powerfully throughout my energy field. I AM now fully recovered, renewed, and restored to perfect health now.

I now fully accept, in consciousness, my perfect recovery from surgery, or better, now. I now give gratitude to God that I AM restored to perfect health now—renewed, restored, and invigorated. I now release this treatment into the Spiritual Law of Perfection Everywhere Now, knowing that it manifests in my life right here and now. Thank you, God, and SO IT IS.

156. Treatment for Perfect, Robust Health

This is a treatment for myself, [*full name*], for my perfect robust health, or better, now.

I recognize that there is one presence and one power at work in the universe and in my life. God is the source of all life. God is the infinite reservoir of cosmic energy. God is the life-giver, the life force energy in the universe. God is the source of eternal, unlimited health, the consummate healer. God is perfect well-being and divine vitality. God is perfection everywhere now. God is perfection here now.

I AM now one with, merged with, and the same as God. God is everywhere, within everything. Therefore God is within me, within this energy field and this body. Thus, God's life-giving eternal health is within me, pervading my entire being. I AM the life force energy, the infinite reservoir of cosmic energy that God is. I AM the perfect well-being and vitality that God is. I AM perfection everywhere now. I AM perfection here now.

I now therefore know and claim for myself, [*full name*], my perfect robust health, or better, now.

I call upon the Holy Spirit, the spirit of wholeness, to bring truth, wisdom, and understanding into my mind now. I now release, dissolve, and let go of any and all limiting thoughts and feelings that no longer serve me. I now dispel from my mind all negative thoughts of guilt, shame, blame, victimization, stress, strain, anxiety, overwhelm, improper diet, improper rest, resentment, blame, self-condemnation, self-punishment, illness, disease, disorder, sickness, infirmity, weakness, and all other thoughts and feelings that have caused ill health in my life, whether known or unknown, conscious or unconscious.

I now know that my health is perfect. I live a healthy lifestyle, with proper rest, nutrition, and exercise, free from stress and strain, or better, now. I now welcome and accept new, positive, powerful healthy thoughts and emotions of forgiveness, self-acceptance, self-accountability, responsibility, calm, stillness, inner peace, relaxation, wellness, well-being, fitness, strength, vigor, vitality, energy, heartiness, vivacity, and perfect robust health, or better, now. My body is in perfect health, right here and now. I AM full of life—healthy, wholesome, vigorous, sound, whole, and complete in every area of my body, mind, emotions, spirit, and life.

I now fully accept, in consciousness, my perfect robust health, or better, now. I now give gratitude to God for my perfect health. I AM healed, whole, well, and sound, right now, in every aspect of my life—physical, mental, emotional, spiritual, and material, or better, now. I now release this prayer into the Spiritual Law, knowing that it does demonstrate in my life, right now. Thank you, God, and SO IT IS.

Magnetizing Love

Love is the master key that opens the gate of happiness.
—Oliver Wendell Holmes

Love is what creates life, maintains life, and nurtures life. It is the magnet that holds the cosmos in place and the glue that makes relationships last. Without love, there is no life. Therefore, we seek love everywhere, and we are motivated by love in our every action. Love is the light of life. It is God manifested on earth.

Every action has love as its motive. Making and maintaining friendships, trying to please your parents, seeking an education, finding a spouse, having children, seeking employment or engaging in a business or profession—these are all done for love. Doing charitable works, gaining patience, expressing compassion, engaging in humanitarian endeavors, seeking spiritual awakening and enlightenment—these are all done for love.

Because love is the motivating factor on this planet, in this chapter, let us now use healing prayers to help you increase love in your life and radiate love vibrations to those around you. You deserve love, and you deserve to be loved. This chapter will help you do that in all of your relations, starting with your relationship with yourself.

157. I AM Lovable Prayer

Seeing yourself as lovable draws loving experiences into your life. Your self-confidence and inner strength grows when you stop judging, condemning, and criticizing yourself.

I celebrate myself. I AM love.
I AM loving and loveable.
I AM infinite beauty.
I AM a child of God, precious in God's eyes.
I love and cherish myself as God loves me.
I like myself unconditionally.
I love myself unconditionally.
I accept myself unconditionally.
I approve of myself unconditionally.
I forgive myself unconditionally.
I trust myself unconditionally.
I bless myself unconditionally.

I allow myself to be my Self.
I AM perfect, complete, and whole.
I AM worthy and deserving of God's good for me.
I AM confident. I AM loved.
Thank you, God, and SO IT IS.

158. The Ocean of God's Love

No love is as vast and profound as God's love. Therefore, when you open to divine love, you are truly, deeply loved and comforted.

I now open my heart to the love that God is.
I now merge into the loving presence of God.
I AM rocked like a baby in the arms of God's love.
I AM soothed and calmed by God's loving presence.
God is the source of comfort that soothes me,
Reassures me, and gives me rest and quietude.
God is the ocean of pure love and infinite peace.
I now bathe in the cosmic ocean of God's love.
The waves of God's liquid love now wash over me,
Reassuring me and bringing me perfect solace.
I AM filled, surrounded, permeated, and pervaded
By the pure, gentle, unconditional love that God is.
I AM the love that God is.
Love dwells within me, as me.
I AM loved, and I AM at peace.
Thank you, God, and SO IT IS.

159. Divine Love Expression

When you allow divine love to express through you, then your life is truly blessed in every way. This prayer will help you experience divine love.

I AM the love that God is. God's love fills my heart.
I AM expressing God's perfect, unconditional love.
I AM always loving in my thoughts, words, and deeds.
I AM patient, kind, gentle, and forgiving.
Harmony and love flood my mind and heart.
I see with divine love, compassion, and understanding.
Divine love, expressing through me,
Now draws to me all that is needed
To make me happy and my life complete.
Divine love draws the people who belong in my life

And unites me with them now.
All people are expressions of divine love;
Therefore, I meet with nothing but expressions of divine love.
Divine love harmonizes; divine love adjusts;
Divine love prospers; divine love foresees everything,
And richly provides every good thing for me now.
Divine love is now victorious. I praise divine love,
Which melts situations and challenges that seem impossible.
Thank you, God, and SO IT IS.

160. I AM Worthy Prayer

When you value yourself as worthy, then you magnetize situations, circumstances, and opportunities for your highest good.

I AM worthy to be loved,
I AM worthy to be prosperous,
I AM worthy to be fulfilled,
I AM worthy to be joyous,
I AM worthy to be abundant,
I AM worthy to be content,
I AM worthy to have a joyous life.
I AM a divine being of great worth.
I like myself, I love myself, I accept myself,
I forgive myself, I trust myself, I believe in myself.
I AM perfect, just as I AM.
I AM lovable, and I AM loved.
Thank you, God, and SO IT IS.

161. Increasing Attractiveness

Attractiveness is more about who you are than what you look like. Though there are physical features often considered beautiful, any person can radiate attractiveness.

My spirit is attractive. My soul is attractive.
My mind is attractive. My body is attractive.
I AM a magnificent being, filled with God's energy;
Therefore I AM attractive.
I now radiate the beauteous light that God is;
Therefore I AM attractive.
I now think, speak, act, and interact lovingly;
Therefore I AM attractive.

My body is a temple of God, and I respect and nurture it;
Therefore, I AM attractive.
I keep my body clean, groomed, and adorned beautifully;
Therefore, I AM attractive.
I keep my mind and emotions clear of all lower energies;
Therefore, I AM attractive.
I AM a people magnet, and I attract love into my life;
Therefore, I AM attractive.
I love life, and life loves me. We get along perfectly together;
Therefore, I AM attractive.
I AM loved.
Thank you, God, and SO IT IS.

162. Increasing Magnetism

The greater your life force energy (known as *prana, chi, or ki),* the more you will radiate, vibrate, and exude magnetism, sex appeal, and charisma.

I AM a beauteous being of love and light.
I radiate God's love and light to everyone around me.
I AM filled with the life force energy that God is.
My energy field emits divine energy and magnetism.
I transmit love by osmosis, and people are drawn to me.
My energy field is glowing, attractive, and charismatic.
I AM magnetic, fascinating, compelling, and captivating.
Love is all around me, and I attract love.
I AM a love magnet. I AM filled with love. I AM loved.
Thank you, God, and SO IT IS.

163. Perfect, Loving Friendships

If you want to have excellent, loyal, faithful, lasting friendships, then you must take time, energy, and dedication to develop them with love and patience.

I AM the love that God is.
I AM the joy that God is.
I AM the friendliness that God is.
I AM the compassion that God is.
I AM the loyalty that God is.
I AM the integrity that God is.
Therefore, I AM a loyal, loving, compassionate friend.

I AM a powerful friend magnet, and that magnet sticks.
Loving friendships come to me effortlessly and naturally.
Loyal friendships stay with me constantly and perpetually.
My life is filled with loving friendships, and I AM fulfilled.
Thank you, God, and SO IT IS.

164. Treatment for Self-Love

This is a treatment for myself, [*full name*], for perfect self-love, or better, now.

I recognize God is divine, unconditional love. God is the source of love. God's perfect love brings peace and content. God is the all-forgiving, the source of compassion, mercy, and understanding. God is the loving parent of this cosmos, and God's perfect work is done through love.

I AM a beloved child of God, held in the arms of God—loved, cherished, and nurtured. Precious in the sight of God, I AM one with God's unconditional love now. God shines the light of forgiveness, mercy, compassion, and understanding upon me now. God's love enfolds me and fills my heart with peace. God's love is doing its perfect work in and through me now. I AM the love that God is.

I therefore claim for myself, [*full name*], perfect self-love, or better, now.

I now heal and release all negative thoughts interfering with this claim, whether known or unknown, conscious or subconscious. My thoughts are now one with, the same as, and in tune with God's thoughts. I dispel from my mind any and all seeming need to punish myself. I let go of all shame, guilt, self-condemnation, embarrassment, and fear of exposure now. I release all fear of making a mistake and not being right.

I now welcome self-love. I AM perfect for me for now. I AM on my perfect path of unfoldment. I forgive myself completely, for I have done the very best I could do in every situation. I have never made a mistake or done anything wrong, for God sees no mistake and no wrong. I AM loved, cherished, and honored in God's eyes.

Nothing in the universe holds anything against me now, and I hold nothing against myself now. I AM a perfect being of divine light, and I surrender all seeming limitations to God. I dispel any and all belief that others are better than, greater than, worse than, or less than myself. I know all beings are equal in the sight of God. I rejoice in God's perfection in every living being. Therefore I like myself, I accept myself, and I forgive myself fully, completely, and unconditionally, right now. I AM perfect exactly the way I AM now.

I welcome God's eternal, ever-flowing, perfect love into my life now, knowing I am immersed and bathed in the ocean of God's love, which is unconditional, boundless, and limitless. God walks with me in love in every moment. I AM loved.

I now fully accept, in consciousness, my perfect self-love, or better, now. I thank God for manifesting this good in my life now, under grace, in God's own wise and perfect ways. I release this treatment fully and completely into the Spiritual Law of Perfection Everywhere Now, knowing it is accepted and demonstrates in my life now, under grace, in perfect ways. SO BE IT.

165. Treatment for Perfect Relationships With Children

This is a treatment for myself, [*full name*], for the perfect loving, respectful relationships with my children, or better, now.

I recognize God is the source of love and respect. God is the ever-loving, all-merciful, all-joyful, everlasting, eternal source of unconditional love and respect now. God is the wellspring of abundant love.

I AM one with God's unconditional love now. I AM unconditional love now. I AM unconditional respect now. I AM a source of constant joy. I AM the love that God is, now and always. I AM the abundance of God's love.

I therefore claim for myself, [*full name*], the perfect loving, respectful relationships with my children, or better, now.

I now heal and release all limiting concepts interfering with this claim, whether known or unknown, conscious or subconscious. My thoughts are now one with, the same as, and in tune with God's thought. I know now my relationships with my children are filled with love and harmony. I dissolve from my mind any thoughts of resentment and fear about my children now. I embrace unconditional love for my children now. I dispel any seeming need to dominate, coerce, or control my children now. I dissolve the need to make all decisions for my children now. I release the idea that only I know what is best for my children. My children are free to follow their own heart, and I AM divinely free to follow my own heart. I dissolve the idea that I possess my children, and I let go of the fear that they will somehow be taken away from me. I know there is no limit to my good, and God is my ever-present supply. Therefore I need not possess anyone or anything. I release my children completely, and I now accept good and joy in all forms from the universe.

I cut any and all psychic ties between myself and my children now. These psychic ties are now lovingly cut, lifted, loved, healed, released, and let go now by the Holy Spirit. I dissolve from my mind any feelings of lack of self-acceptance, lack of self-love, and lack of self-worth now. They are now let go, loosed, and released by God's divine light. I accept myself the way I AM, and I AM free to express my Self the way I AM. I accept my children the way they are, and they are free to express themselves the way they are. I AM the perfection of God in human form, and I AM perfect for me for now. My children are also perfect for them for now. I AM filled with self-love, self-acceptance, and self-worth now. I AM free to love and respect my children now and I accept their love and respect now.

I fully accept, in consciousness, my perfect loving, respectful relationships with my children, or better, now. I thank God for manifesting loving relationships with my children now, under grace, in perfect ways. Thank you, God, and SO IT IS.

166. Treatment for Perfect Relationship With Parents

This is a treatment for myself, [*full name*], for the perfect loving relationship with my parents, or better, now.

I recognize that God is the everlasting, unbounded source of love. God is perfect love. God is wholeness, oneness, and peace. God is eternal harmony and joy. God is the source of humility, gratitude, and thanksgiving now.

I AM one with God's everlasting, unbounded love. God loves me unconditionally now and at all times. I AM wholeness, oneness, and peace. God's eternal harmony and joy saturate my life now. I AM filled with thanksgiving, gratitude, and humility now in the face of God's infinite love.

I therefore claim for myself, [*full name*], my perfect loving relationship with my parents, or better, now.

I now heal and release all negative beliefs interfering with this claim, whether known or unknown, conscious or subconscious. My thoughts are now one with, the same as, and in tune with God's thought. I accept, in consciousness, that my relationship with my parents is healed and forgiven now. I dispel from my mind any and all feelings of unworthiness and guilt concerning my parents now. I dissolve all judgment toward my parents now. I release all beliefs that my parents are criticizing me now. I release all feelings of anger and resentment toward my parents now. I let go of the thought that my parents need to change in any way.

I now embrace the knowledge that my parents are perfect the way they are. I now accept my parents exactly the way they are without attempting to change them. I AM filled with self-worth, self-acceptance, and forgiveness of my parents now. I know they did the best they could in every situation with me, and I did the best I could in every situation with them. Therefore, there is no guilt or blame. I forgive myself completely, and I love my parents unconditionally now.

I free my parents to express themselves in their own unique way, and I free myself to express in my own individual way.

I call upon the Holy Spirit to cut all psychic ties between my parents and myself now. These psychic ties are now lovingly cut, lifted, loved, healed, released, and let go in the name of God. I AM free to love my parents with God's perfect love now.

I now fully accept, in consciousness, my perfect loving relationship with my parents, or better, now. I thank God for manifesting this good in my life now. Thank you, God, and SO IT IS.

167. Treatment to Attract Perfect Mate and Companion

This is a treatment for myself, [*full name*], for my perfect mate and companion with compatible likes, interests, desires, appetites, values, purpose, career, and ideals, or better, to be with me in an intimate, committed, monogamous relationship now. This perfect mate is compatible with me in every way—spiritually, emotionally, socially, morally, intellectually, mentally, geographically, financially, physically, and sexually, or better, now.

I recognize that God is all-loving, the wellspring of love, the fountain of good, the river of strength. God is the incarnation of divine love, the one true source of unconditional love. God is perfect fulfillment, contentment, and joy. God sees love and perfection in every particle of creation.

God is the fountain of my good, the river of my strength. God fills and surrounds me with love now. God's love opens my heart to all joy and blessings. I AM the contentment and fulfillment that God is now. I AM one with the source of love: God the good, the omnipotent. I AM filled with unconditional divine love now. I AM created in the likeness and image of God. Thus, I AM a child of God, and God loves me exactly the way I AM.

I therefore claim for myself, [*full name*], my perfect mate and companion, with compatible likes, interests, desires, appetites, values, purpose, career, and ideals, or better, to be with me in an intimate, committed, monogamous relationship, or better, now. This perfect mate is compatible with me in every way—spiritually, emotionally, socially, morally, intellectually, mentally, geographically, financially, physically, and sexually, or better, now.

I fully accept my perfect mate, in consciousness, now. I now heal and release all negative ideas interfering with this claim, whether known or unknown, conscious or subconscious. My thoughts are now one with, the same as, and in tune with God's thoughts. I dispel from my mind now any and all thoughts of unworthiness, fear of intimacy, fear of abandonment, fear of rejection, sadness, bitterness, resentment, anger toward the opposite sex, and negative memories of past relationships. I give these thoughts over to the Holy Spirit now.

I now wholeheartedly accept in my life unconditional love, peace, intimacy, self-love, self-acceptance, self-worth, fulfillment, inner strength, self-authority, forgiveness of past relationships, forgiveness of the opposite sex, forgiveness of all past memories.

I call upon the Holy Spirit to cut all psychic ties between myself and all past memories of relationships now. I also cut all psychic ties between myself and all past romantic attachments now. All these psychic ties are now lovingly cut, lifted, loved, healed, released, and let go in the name of God. I AM free of these past experiences and free to welcome my perfect mate into my life now.

I now fully accept, in consciousness, my perfect mate and companion, or better, now, under grace in perfect ways. I thank God for manifesting my perfect mate now. Thank you, God, and SO IT IS.

168. Treatment for Happy, Harmonious Marriage

This is a treatment for myself, [*full name*], for my perfect loving, harmonious marriage, or better, now.

I now recognize there is one loving power and one loving presence at work in the universe and in my life: God, the good, the omnipotent. God is pure love, free from conditions, judgments, and condemnation. God is all-merciful, all-compassionate, all-embracing, and all-encompassing. God is the source of forgiveness and gratitude. God is wholeness and oneness. God is perfect harmony, joy, and happiness.

I AM now one with God. God is within me and all around me. For in God I live, breathe, move, and have my being. I AM united with and merged with God in a perfect seamless wholeness. God is the very center and essence of my being. I AM the unconditional love that God is. I AM the mercy, compassion, acceptance, and inclusion that God is. I AM the forgiveness, gratitude, wholeness, oneness, harmony, joy, and happiness that God is.

I now therefore know and claim for myself, [*full name*], my perfect, loving, harmonious marriage, or better, now.

I now release, loose, and let go of anything that interferes with my perfect, loving, harmonious marriage, whether known or unknown, conscious or unconscious. I now call upon the Holy Spirit, the spirit of truth and wholeness, to release from my mind any and all thoughts of control, coercion, criticism, judgment, contempt, anger, resentment, fear, frustration, impatience, guilt, shame, blame, unworthiness, lack, incompleteness, dissatisfaction, and disillusionment. These thoughts are all lifted, healed, loved, dissolved, released, and completely let go. And they are gone.

I now welcome into my heart and mind positive, creative, beauteous thoughts of letting go, permissiveness, forgiveness, compassion, mercy, acceptance, appreciation, kindness, gentleness, wisdom, courage, faith, trust, patience, forbearance, worthiness, abundance, completeness, contentment, satisfaction, guilelessness, and innocence.

I now cut any and all psychic ties between myself and my spouse. These psychic ties are now lovingly cut, cut, cut, cut, cut, cut, cut, cut, cut, cut, cut, cut, cut, cut, cut, cut, cut, cut, cut, cut, cut, cut, cut, cut, lifted, loved, healed, dissolved, released, and completely let go, into the light of God's love and truth. I now know I AM free to be myself, and my spouse is free to be himself/herself.

I now know I have a happy, harmonious marriage, based upon mutual trust, understanding, love, gratitude, respect, patience, humility, and forgiveness. I know now my relationship with my spouse is filled with love, harmony, and joy. I now give sincere gratitude to God for my spouse and for my marriage.

I now fully accept, in consciousness, my perfect, loving, harmonious marriage, or better, now. I now release this prayer into the Spiritual Law, knowing it does demonstrate right now, under God's love and grace, in perfect ways. Thank you, God, and SO BE IT.

169. Treatment for Harmonious Home Life

This is a treatment for myself, [*full name*], for the perfect loving, peaceful, harmonious home life and family relationships, or better, now.

I recognize there is one source of harmony, peace, and love in the universe: God, the good, omnipotent and omnipresent. God is perfect unity, the wellspring of rest and continual renewal. God is the safe haven of peace.

I AM one with this source of good, harmony, love, and peace now. God is my one power and the source of unity for my life now. I AM an instrument of God's peace and harmony in my home. At home in God's safe haven, I find rest and renewal every day.

I therefore claim for myself, [*full name*], the perfect loving, peaceful, harmonious home life and family relationships, or better, now.

I now heal and release all negations from my mind that interfere with this claim, whether known or unknown, conscious or subconscious. My thoughts are now one with, the same as, and in tune with God's thought. I now cut all psychic ties between myself and those who live with me. These psychic ties are now lovingly cut, lifted, loved, healed, released, and let go into the light of God's love.

I know any dear ones influencing my home are now bless-ed, forgiven, and released into the love, light, and wholeness of divinity. You are unified with your true nature of being. God's love and light fill and surround you now with love and peace. The earth no longer binds you. Fear and blame no longer keep you in chains. I call upon your higher Self to take you into the light of God now. Go now in peace and love.

I AM now free from all attachments that have prevented unconditional love in my homelife and family relationships now. I call upon the divine presence to dissolve from my mind all feelings of resentment, fear, coercion, domination, sadness, pain, rejection, and abandonment. They are released and healed by divine wisdom now. I instead welcome into my home and family new feelings of love, happiness, forgiveness, freedom, self-authority, joy, healing, self-love, self-acceptance, and self-worth now. I now free all persons in my home to express themselves in their own unique and perfect way, and I AM free to express, in my own perfect way. I see only good in myself and in them.

I now fully accept, in consciousness, harmony, peace, and love, or better, in my home and in my family now. I now thank God for answered prayer. Thank you, God, and SO IT IS.

170. Treatment for Sexual Fulfillment

This is a treatment for myself, [*full name*], for my perfect sexual fulfillment, or better, now, with my consenting adult partner in a joyous, loving relationship.

I recognize that God is the source of pleasure and fulfillment, the wellspring of satisfaction. God is unconditional love, acceptance, joy, and happiness. God is the source of pure love and is free from judgment. God is the full expression of unconditional love, now and always.

I AM one with God's love and non-judging acceptance now. God's full expression of love permeates my life now. God's joy and happiness flood my heart with fullness. I AM replete with the pleasure of God's garden of joy and delight now. I AM unconditional love now.

I therefore claim for myself, [*full name*], my perfect sexual fulfillment, or better, now, with my consenting adult partner in a joyous, loving relationship.

I now heal and release all negations that interfere with this claim, whether known or unknown, conscious or subconscious. My thoughts are now one with, the same as, and in tune with God's thought. I dissolve from my mind any and all ideas of limitation, inhibition, fear, disgust, frustration, sexual guilt, and self-hatred now. And they are gone.

I now welcome and accept freedom of expression, joy, uninhibitedness, love, fullness, fulfillment, forgiveness of self, and self-love now. I now release all negative ideas about sex from my upbringing. I release any ideas that sex is bad, dirty, or harmful. I now accept that sex is a beautiful, joyful expression of love. I now accept there is nothing wrong with my safe sexual expression with my consenting adult partner.

I cut any and all psychic ties between myself and anyone who has made me feel guilty about sex. I cut, lift, love, heal, release, and let go of these psychic ties now, and they are dissolved in God's love and light. I now fully accept my beautiful body and my sexual expression with my consenting adult partner. I AM a loving, sexual, beautiful being of God, and my love is expressed sexually now in great joy and fulfillment. I AM filled with the joyous freedom of sexual pleasure and satisfaction now. My sexual expression is the expression of divine love. I AM perfect exactly the way I AM now, and I express my Self freely the way I AM now.

I now fully accept, in consciousness, my perfect sexual fulfillment, or better, now, with my consenting adult partner in a joyous loving relationship. I thank God for manifesting this good in my life now under grace in perfect ways. Thank you, God, and SO IT IS.

Attracting Prosperity

When you focus on being a blessing, God makes sure that you are always blessed in abundance.
—Joel Osteen

As you think, so you become. Whatever you place attention upon grows stronger in your life. If your thoughts, speech, and actions are focused on prosperity, you become prosperous. However, seeking wealth for its own sake can be a lonely, unsatisfying endeavor. Discovering your true life purpose and divine plan, and then manifesting that in a prosperous way, is the key to abundance that inspires yourself, lifts others, and blesses the entire planet.

Many spiritual people seem allergic to riches and wealth. They believe the wealthy can never be spiritual. In a contest between spirituality and riches, any person of faith would choose spirituality. However, could you possibly conceive there is no contest? My experience in 45 years of spiritual teaching is that money, or lack thereof, has nothing to do with your state of awareness or spiritual evolution.

The truth is that money is energy. It can be used for good. Using the affirmations and prayers in this chapter can help you manifest more prosperity for yourself and your family.

171. Prosperity Prayer

You deserve prosperity, and you can have it by affirming and knowing your heavenly Mother/Father God is the source of your supply.

Divine love, through me, blesses and multiplies
All that I AM, all that I have,
All that I give, and all that I receive.
Everyone and everything prospers me now.
I AM a child of God, created in God's likeness.
My birthright is infinite abundance.
Therefore I inherit unlimited wealth.
God is the source of my supply
And provides abundantly for me now.
I prosper and succeed in every area of my life.
All my needs are met. In God, I have no lack.
God is my divine banker and financial advisor.
God is in charge of all my financial affairs,

And provides all my needs and wants, right now.
Thank you, God, and SO IT IS.

172. God's Plenty

Many people block their prosperity by believing money is limited, and there is not enough to go around. That false belief must be reversed if you want abundance. This prayer can help.

There is plenty for everyone, including myself.
I AM enriched and fulfilled,
Divinely directed and lavishly prospered,
Through the unlimited goodness of God.
I AM thriving, wealthy, and affluent, within and without.
My good is now flowing to me so richly and fully
That I have an abundance of money to spare and share.
God's good circulates freely through my life
And prospers me mightily, right now.
God is my unfailing source of supply,
And large sums of money now come to me quickly.
I live on an unlimited income.
Success and prosperity come easily to me,
Right now and always, eternally sustained.
Thank you, God, and SO IT IS.

173. My Purpose and Prosperity

When your actions are aligned and attuned with your divine purpose, then you will prosper. You will be given all you need to fulfill that divine plan.

My individual and divine purpose are one,
Unfolding beautifully and comfortably
According to God's perfect wisdom and grace.
My prosperity manifests and flows
To support me and my purpose in every way.
My prosperity comes completely in freedom
As a gift of God's grace.
I AM worthy to receive prosperity.
I love myself fully and completely.
Thank you, God, and SO IT IS.

174. Gratitude for God's Bounty

Gratitude is an essential ingredient for prosperity. However, this prayer goes a step further. It is about aligning your human will to the will of God.

All that I AM, all that I have, and all that I intend
Is created, maintained, and eternally sustained
By the gift of grace that is God.
I now give gratitude and thanksgiving
For the bounty that is bestowed upon me
By the heavenly Mother/Father God,
Whose rain falls upon all eternally and abundantly.
Thank you, wonderful God, for all you are.
You are my source of inspiration,
The lighthouse of my life, the very breath of my being.
I cling to you as my redeemer, my comforter,
My safe haven of nourishment and protection.
I belong to you. I AM yours.
Thank you, God, and SO IT IS.

175. Fountainhead of Wealth

In India, Lakshmi is the goddess of wealth. She is an eternal fountainhead of riches, and she bestows wealth liberally to those who invoke her with faith.

I call upon the great goddess Lakshmi,
The heavenly bestower of wealth and happiness,
To pour forth your fountainhead of infinite riches
In a bliss-bestowing, boundless stream.
An eternal waterfall of prosperity and plenty
Now cascades its fortune into my being.
A cornucopia of ever-flowing bounty
Now rushes into my life with limitless wealth.
I AM blessed with unceasing good fortune,
Opulence, money, affluence, and assets,
Now and forevermore.
Everything I touch now turns to gold.
Thank you, God, and SO IT IS.

176. Infinite Substance and Supply

God, the source and creator of everything, is an infinite storehouse of divine substance that can be drawn upon to materialize anything.

I AM now one with, merged with, and the same as
The infinite substance, the source of all supply.
My mind and heart unite in gratitude with precise purpose
To tap into the infinite substance and to manifest my good.
Whatever my mind conceives and my heart believes,

I now achieve—easily, naturally, and purposefully.
I now effortlessly materialize all my heart's desires,
As I draw upon God's unlimited substance and supply.
God always says yes to every heartfelt request.
With faith and trust in God, all things are possible.
Thank you, God, and SO IT IS.

177. Money Magnet Affirmation

Some people seem to attract money like a magnet. You can become one of those people by affirming that you are.

I AM a money magnet.
I love money and money loves me.
It comes to me often and stays with me.
I AM a money magnet.
I love money and money loves me.
It sticks to me now and ever increases.
I AM a money magnet.
I love money and money loves me.
Money is my friend, and it is always with me.
It increases more and more, and I welcome it.
I AM a money magnet,
And I AM grateful to God.
Thank you, God, and SO IT IS.

178. Divine Work Expression

This prayer can help you create and maintain an ideal work position, where your true skills, talents, and abilities are joyously expressed, and where you attain success through completing your tasks with excellence.

My perfect position with my perfect salary
Now manifests in God's own perfect time and way.
My income is constantly increasing.
Promotions come easily to me.
I always give 100 percent at work,
And I AM greatly appreciated.
My work is fulfilling, joyous, and satisfying.
Remaining focused and alert, I do my work
Efficiently, effortlessly, effectively, accurately, and on time.
I think clearly, concisely, and correctly
In all tasks that are set before me.
My workspace is a pleasure to be in.

I AM harmonious with all my coworkers
In an atmosphere of mutual respect.
My business is expanding beyond my expectations.
I always attract the best customers,
And they are a joy to serve.
I attract all the business I can comfortably handle.
Thank you, God, and SO IT IS.

179. Treatment for Perfect Abundance

This is a treatment for myself, [*full name*], for the perfect divine abundance and prosperity, or better, manifesting in my life now.

I recognize that God is the cornucopia of abundance, the source of money, wealth, and prosperity. God is the fountainhead of all riches, divine unlimited bounty, and fulfillment. God is the reservoir of goodness, flowing in an eternal stream. God is the divine banker and supreme benefactor. God is the infinite source of all blessings, and there is always a divine surplus. God's measureless wealth circulates freely throughout the cosmos.

I AM one with God's neverending flow of abundance now. God pours money, wealth, and prosperity upon me now in an endless stream. God's wellspring of limitless bounty floods into my life now. I AM filled to the brim and overflowing with plenty. I AM enriched and fulfilled through the infinite goodness of God. God is my divine banker. I AM the wealthy beneficiary of a loving God, and wealth is perpetually circulating throughout my life. God's love, through me, blesses and multiplies all that I have, all that I give, and all that I receive.

I therefore claim for myself, [*full name*], perfect divine abundance and prosperity, or better, manifesting in my life now.

I AM one with God's divine mind now. My thoughts are one with God's thoughts. I now release all negative thoughts that have blocked me from my unlimited divine bounty and prosperity now. I now release all ideas that money is evil and that wealthy people are materialistic and non-spiritual. I let go of the idea that spiritual people are meant to be poor. I now release all ideas of being unworthy or undeserving of abundance. All these limiting thoughts are now lifted into divine light and let go by God's love.

I now freely welcome the idea that I AM worthy of abundance, that prosperity is mine. I embrace thoughts that money is energy, money is good, money is spiritual, and a wealthy person can be Godly, divinely guided, and inspired. I therefore open my arms to receive the abundance of divine wealth now. I AM overflowing with the abundance of joy, love, money, and wealth now. Money, gems, jewels, luxuries, possessions, assets, cash, and checks are showered upon me now. God's infinite wealth fills my bank account now and provides an unending source of credit. I place my bank account in God's hands, and God writes all my checks.

I AM therefore now linked to an unlimited source of wealth and continual circulation of prosperity. I have all the wealth, money, assets, and riches I could ever need. I circulate this wealth freely now. The abundant good and bounty of the universe is manifesting in my financial affairs now. There is no limit to my good, which is now flowing to me so richly and fully that I have a surplus of money to spare and share. I receive the abundant good that is mine by divine right now. Everything and everyone prosper me now, and I prosper everyone and everything now. I AM the wealthy beneficiary of a loving God, so I dare to prosper, right here and now.

I now fully accept, in consciousness, my perfect divine abundance and prosperity or better manifesting in my life now. I thank God for unlimited wealth and prosperity. I thank God that this is so now, and SO IT IS.

180. Prayer for Getting Rich

This prayer is based upon by the New Thought classic *The Science of Getting Rich,* by Wallace D. Wattles (1860–1911).

There is a thinking stuff, from which all things are made, and which, in its original state, permeates, penetrates, and fills the interspaces of the universe. A thought in this substance produces the thing that is imaged by the thought.

I now form things in my thought, and by impressing my thought upon formless substance, I now cause the thing that I think about to be created. As I do this, I now pass from the competitive to the creative mind, so I AM in harmony with formless intelligence, which is always creative and never competitive in spirit.

I now come into full harmony with the formless substance by entertaining a lively and sincere gratitude for the blessings it bestows upon me. Gratitude unifies my mind with the intelligence of substance, and my thoughts are now received by the formless. I now remain upon the creative plane by uniting myself with the formless intelligence through a deep and continuous feeling of gratitude.

I now form a clear and definite mental image of the thing I wish to have, to do, or to become, and I now hold this mental image in my thoughts, while being deeply grateful to the supreme that all my desires are granted to me. I now spend my leisure hours in contemplating my vision, and in earnest thanksgiving that the reality is being given to me. I now frequently contemplate my clear mental image, coupled with unwaivering faith and devout gratitude.

This is the process by which the impression is given to the formless and the creative forces are set in motion. The creative energy works through the established channels of natural growth, and of the industrial and social order. All that is included in my mental image is surely brought to me, for as I follow these instructions, my faith does not waver. What I want now comes to me through the ways of established trade and commerce.

In order to receive my own when it is ready to come to me, I act in a way that causes me to more than fill my present place. I now keep in mind the purpose to get rich through realization of my mental image. And I now do, every day, all that can be done that day, taking care to do each act in a successful manner. I now give to every person a use value in excess of the cash value he or she receives, so each transaction makes for more life, and I now hold the advancing thought so the impression of increase is now communicated to all with whom I come into contact.

I now give gratitude to God for manifesting riches into my life, under grace, in perfect ways. I now release this prayer into divine substance, which accepts it and manifests it now, under grace, in perfect ways. Thank you, wonderful God, and SO IT IS.

181. Treatment for Perfect Income

This is a treatment for myself, [*full name*], for the perfect net income of [*amount*] per month, or better, now.

I recognize that God is the source of all abundance and prosperity in the universe. God is the fountain of all bounty, all strength, and all good. God is the wish-fulfilling tree, the generous provider of all blessings and boons.

God's good is my good now. I welcome and accept God's blessings in my life now. God's bounty is mine now. There is no separation between God and myself; therefore a never-ending fountainhead of abundance flows freely into my life now with divine order and timing.

I now claim for myself, [*full name*], my perfect net income of [*amount*] per month, or better, now.

I accept, in consciousness, this perfect income now. I dissolve from my mind all limitations preventing me from having all perfect sources of income now, whether these limitations are known or unknown, conscious or subconscious. My mind is united with divine mind now. I therefore accept all perfect sources of income for myself now, including unexpected sources. I release all limiting beliefs of denial of income from any avenues now, of not being worthy to receive my good, and of not deserving prosperity. I dispel all beliefs that wealth is not spiritual and money is the root of evil. All these thoughts are now lifted into God's love and released into divine light.

I now know in my mind that money is divine, it can be used for good, and I AM worthy and deserving to receive wealth and abundance. I know God's immeasurable bounty flows into my life in a perpetual stream, without restriction. I open my mind and heart to all avenues of wealth, income, and abundance, even those I previously never considered. I AM willing and open now to receive prosperity. My life is blessed with the free-flowing continual circulation of wealth and riches right now.

I now fully accept, in consciousness, my divine abundance now in the form of my net income of [*amount*] per month, or better, now. I thank God for answered prayer. I thank God for my perfect sources of income now, under grace, in perfect ways. I release this treatment into the Spiritual Law, knowing it demonstrates now. Thank you, God, and SO IT IS.

182. Treatment for Perfect Employment

This is a treatment for myself, [*full name*], for the perfect employment for myself now, with a salary of [*amount*] per week, or better, which uses all of my talents and strengths of [*talents*] or better, and which I love doing now.

I recognize God is the divine employer. God's will is at work in the universe and God's purpose is present within everyone and everything. God is the source of strength and the source of power. God is the generous benefactor of all life in this universe.

God is my divine employer now. God's divine will is at work in my life now. God's will is my will now. I AM in tune with my divine life purpose, which reflects my true desires and true pathway now. I AM one with God's power and strength now. I AM open, receptive, and faithful to God's perfect divine plan for my life. I AM the beneficiary of God's good will now.

I therefore claim for myself, [*full name*], the perfect employment for myself now, with a salary of [*amount*] per week, or better, which utilizes all my talents and strengths of [*talents*], or better, and which I love doing now.

I now accept, in consciousness, this perfect employment now. I now heal and release all thoughts that interfere with this claim, whether known or unknown, conscious or subconscious. My thoughts are now one with, the same as, and in tune with God's thoughts. I now free my mind and heart from any and all thoughts of unworthiness, lack, limitation, frustration, and fear. They are now dissolved by the light of God's love. I dispel and renounce from my mind now any and all beliefs that I cannot find employment that I love and that uses my strengths and talents.

I now open my mind to ideas of worthiness, abundance, prosperity, strength, ease, joy, fun, loving my job, being happy in my job, and finding the perfect employment for myself that uses my talents and strengths, or better.

I now cut any and all psychic ties between myself and all previous jobs I have had. These psychic ties are now lovingly cut, lifted, loved, healed, released, and let go by the power and the presence of God. I AM attuned to divine order and divine timing in finding my perfect employment now. God is my perfect employer now, and God now bestows upon me my perfect job in the perfect situation in my perfect career path, or better, now.

I now fully accept, in consciousness, my perfect employment, or better, now. Thank you, God, for using me to fulfill your wonderful purpose for me now. I thank God for this perfect employment manifesting in my life now. Thank you, God, and SO IT IS.

183. Treatment for Perfect Housing

This is a treatment for myself, [*full name*], for the perfect housing for myself now in a comfortable and spacious home with [*number*] bedrooms and [*number*] bathrooms, and [*list other features*], in [*place*], or better, which is easily affordable for me, and which suits all my needs, or better, now.

I recognize God is the only power and presence at work in the universe. God's perfect stability, prosperity, joy, and abundance fill the cosmos with divine love. God is the safe haven and perfect shelter from all storms.

I AM one with God now. God's holy sanctuary within my heart is the perfect place for me to reside. God is my only dwelling place. Right where I AM, I AM at home in the presence of God. The temple of God's love rests within my heart, and I AM secure in God's love. God's prosperity, abundance, and joy fulfill my life now. I AM safe in God's perfect haven of love and shelter.

I therefore claim for myself, [*full name*], the perfect housing for myself now in a comfortable, spacious home with [*number*] bedrooms and [*number*] bathrooms in [*place*], and [*list other features*], which is easily affordable for me, and which suits all my needs, or better, now.

I now accept, in consciousness, this perfect place to live. I now heal and release all negative beliefs that interfere with this claim, whether known or unknown, conscious or subconscious. My thoughts are now one with, the same as, and in tune with God's thoughts. I denounce and dissolve from my mind any thoughts preventing me from accepting this perfect home now. I release all thoughts of fear, insecurity, unworthiness, instability, lack of commitment, guilt, sadness, and pain now. I now open my heart to embrace love, hope, faith, happiness, stability, commitment, fulfillment, forgiveness of self, and joy.

I release all psychic ties and attachments with any previous dwelling-places I have lived in. These psychic ties are now cut, lifted, loved, healed, released, and let go by the power of the Holy Spirit. I AM in control of my mind now. I welcome with open arms my perfect, beautiful home, or better, now.

I thank my perfect home for sheltering me so comfortably. Every nook and cranny in it is inviting. My heart is at home in my perfect house. Everyone who enters into my home feels the warmth and love of God.

I now fully accept, in consciousness, the perfect housing for myself, or better, now. I thank God for manifesting this home in my life now, under grace, in God's own wise and perfect ways. Thank you, God, and SO BE IT.

184. Treatment for a Perfect Vehicle

This is a treatment for myself, [*full name*], for the perfect vehicle with [*number*] doors, mechanically sound, safe, comfortable, enjoyable to drive, fuel-efficient, easily affordable for me, operating perfectly, and [*list other features*], or better, now.

I recognize God is the source of all abundance in the universe. God is the one power and the one presence that manifests all good now. God is the source of all creation. God is good, very good perfection now.

I AM one with the source of creation now. God is my ever-bountiful source of prosperity now. God is my unfailing ever-present fountainhead of bounty now. I AM one with my good, very good perfection now.

I therefore claim for myself, [*full name*], the perfect vehicle with [*number*] doors, mechanically sound, safe, comfortable, enjoyable to drive, fuel efficient, easily affordable for me, operating perfectly, and [*list other features*], or better, now.

I accept my perfect vehicle now, and I heal and release all old beliefs and thoughts that interfere with this claim, whether known or unknown, conscious or subconscious. My thoughts are now one with, the same as, and in tune with God's thought. I let go of all thoughts of fear, resistance, guilt, blame, confusion, and lack from my mind now. I dissolve from my mind all belief that I do not deserve the vehicle of my dreams now.

I know I deserve my wonderful new vehicle now. I embrace thoughts of love, acceptance, abundance, forgiveness of self, openness to receive, divine order, and prosperity now. I now let go of all vehicles I have owned in the past, knowing the past is gone and today is a new day of God's fresh, joyous opportunities and possibilities. With God as my wish-bestowing tree, I know the perfect vehicle of my dreams manifests now. My vehicle is ready to go whenever I AM. Driving is a safe and pleasant experience for me and those who ride with me. My mechanic does a good job for a fair price.

I now fully accept, in consciousness, and welcome my perfect vehicle, or better, now. I thank God for manifesting this good in my life now in perfect ways. Thank you, God and SO IT IS.

Making Life a Success

Success doesn't come the way you think it does;
it comes from the way you think.
—Robert Schuller

Does money, wealth, riches, fame, or celebrity make you successful? Or is success a more intangible commodity? Dale Carnegie said, "Success is getting what you want. Happiness is wanting what you get." Real success can only come when you are content with your life, and when you have accepted what is, right now.

There is only one thing blocking your success: your own mind. When you create obstacles with self-sabotaging thoughts, you get in your own way. Materialization of success is entirely determined by how you accept success. If you welcome it with open heart and mind, it comes effortlessly. If, on the other hand, you unconsciously fight success, your fuzzy intention produces fuzzy results.

In general, spiritual people are not prone to welcome success, because it conjures materialistic images. Those with spiritual aspirations often lean toward non-materialism. However, if you were to reframe the idea of success, you might find it means discovering your true Self and expressing who you really are.

True success comes by realizing the ultimate truth of life and attaining spiritual awakening and enlightenment. But those who have realized this higher consciousness did not stumble upon it by accident. They achieved it though lifetimes of patient spiritual practice, self-discipline, and focused intention.

The affirmations and prayers in his chapter can help you attain whatever brand of success you are searching for, whether materialistic, non-materialistic, or transcendental.

185. All Possibilities With God

What seem to be impossible miraculous achievements can be attained with God as your ally. Your life can be graced with miracles each day.

With God, all things are possible.
God is the source of endless blessings and infinite possibilities.
The continuous stream of substance
Flows into my hands from expected and unexpected sources.

Each day holds the promise of new achievements.
Every day is God's new opportunity.
Yesterday is over and done.
Today is the first new day of God's blessings.
Every day is an ever-fresh world of endless
Possibilities, wonders, and miracles.
I walk in the charmed circle of God's love.
In my life, every moment is a miracle.
Thank you, God, and SO IT IS.

186. Highest Good

When you pray for highest good for yourself and all others, without specifying particular goals, you attract great blessings, grace, and miracles.

I now recognize all is God and all is good.
I now know God is good and only good.
I now welcome all of God's good for me.
I now accept my good and only good.
I AM divinely irresistible to my highest good now.
My good comes in good measure,
Pressed down, shaken together, and running over.
My life is filled to the brim
And overflowing with abundant good.
God is incapable of separation or division.
Therefore, my good is incapable of separation or division.
I AM one with my undivided good, now.
God is good, very good perfection now.
I claim my good, very good perfection now,
And eternally sustained.
I now bless everyone, everything,
And every situation in my life,
As good, good, and very good.
I now welcome my good, knowing I AM fulfilled.
I accept the highest good for myself,
And all others concerned.
Thank you, God, and SO IT IS.

187. God's Blessings

By claiming unlimited blessings and infinite possibilities, you expect your life to be graced with success, and that is exactly what happens.

My soul awakens to new blessings of God's love and grace.
I AM attuned to the blessings of answered prayer now.
I claim my blessings now.
Every cell in my body is saturated with blessings.
I share these blessings with all,
And rejoice that I now live life fully.
God has created for me a world
Rich with endless blessings, infinite possibilities,
And unlimited opportunities.
I AM blessed as I share the light of Spirit within me.
I expect the best and I say yes
To all the good and wonderful blessings coming to me.
Thank you, God, and SO IT IS.

188. God's Grace

God's grace is an experience of spiritual nourishment, which brings inspiration and inner strength. With divine grace, you can weather any storm.

I give thanks for grace, a sacred gift from God.
The grace of God is divine love in action.
Grace is the love of God that uplifts, strengthens,
And encourages me daily.
Through the love of God,
I AM living in the eternal grace of God.
The grace of God sustains and fulfills me.
The grace of God blesses me all the days of my life.
Thank you, God, and SO IT IS.

189. Perfect, Right Intention and Perfect, Right Results

When your life is lived in your highest good, and aligned with the laws of nature, you are blessed by the grace of good fortune and countless miracles.

I AM in the perfect, right place at the perfect, right time,
Doing the perfect, right actions in the perfect, right way,
Manifesting perfect, divine, right results.
I now manifest my perfect, right intention,
And live my life of divine synchronicity.
I AM joy, beauty, radiance, freedom, love,
And perfection, on all levels of being.
I AM lucky, and I attract good fortune.

My life is filled with wonders and miracles.
Thank you, God, and SO IT IS.

190. Unlimited Life, Energy, and Freedom

Life can be joyous, full, fun, and free when you express unlimited creative expression, passion, and enthusiasm.

I AM unlimited and free as God created me to be.
I breathe deeply of the breath of life and the freedom of Spirit.
I AM a free Spirit—free in mind, body, and soul.
I AM a radiating center of divine life,
And I give my life full and free expression.
God's love in me is drawing to me
New ideas, new courage, and visible daily supply.
I AM alive, alert, awake, joyous, and excited about life.
I AM filled with energy, passion, and enthusiasm.
Spirit guides me to fresh, new opportunities.
Every moment of every day is brimming
With unlimited possibilities.
Thank you, God, and SO IT IS.

191. Letting Go of Expectations

You have control over what you think, say, and do at the present moment. However, you do not have control over future results. Therefore, let go of all expectations concerning the fruits of your actions.

My mind is now fully merged with the divine mind,
The perfect expression of my Self as divine beingness.
Divine inspiration guides my actions, reactions, and results.
I relinquish control of my life to the Holy Spirit.
By releasing and letting go of the false ego,
I now know my highest good is manifest
On all levels of expression and experience,
In perfect, divine order, perfect, divine timing,
In the perfect, right way, manifesting divine results.
I have no attachment to results.
I now accept the highest good on all levels of being.
I now release all results into divine knowing.
I now embrace inner truth and inner wisdom.
Thank you, God, and SO IT IS.

192. Let Go and Let God

By surrendering to the will of God, your life takes on new meaning and tenor. Your life becomes extraordinary, blessed with marvels and synchronous events.

I let go and I let God show me the way.
I let go and let God direct and manage my life.
I let go and let God work wonders in my life.
I let go and I let God do the work through me.
I let go of all and I let God handle it all.
I do God's will in all the little things in my life.
I do not wait for big things.
I allow God's will to be done in all things.
I now release all into God's care.
I lay down every weight and burden.
God's will for me is good and only good.
I AM an idea in the mind of God.
I let God's idea express in me. I AM the mind of God.
I AM doing God's will. I do the work of God.
God cannot fail. Therefore, I cannot fail.
God is in charge of my life and affairs beyond my human efforts.
Thy will be done on earth, as it is in heaven.
Thank you, God, and SO IT IS.

193. Perfect Expression of God in Action

You are an expression of God. When you reveal who you really are, your life becomes meaningful beyond all human conditions and limitations. You become a gift of perfect divine grace.

I now know God is infinite and eternal love,
Divine grace, pure and perfect beauty,
Divine process, divine results,
Perfection everywhere present now, and eternally sustained.
I AM the perfect expression of all that God is.
In, and through, and as, all life.
I AM one with beautiful, wonderful
God, Goddess, love, and light.
I AM God in action, God in activity, God's philanthropist.
I now go with, and live with, in, and through
The divine flow, which moves within and all around me.

I AM a being of light, a body of light.
My word is the perfect expression
Of my wisdom, my Self, and my inspiration.
Thank you, God, and SO IT IS.

194. Discovering My Divine Plan and Purpose

Everyone's life has a true divine plan, purpose, meaning, and mission. With this prayer, you can begin to discover yours.

My life is purposeful. My life is meaningful.
I now know I have a true divine mission.
My divine plan and purpose are revealed to me,
Easily, effortlessly, and in divine order and timing.
I now open to realize and to achieve
The true divine plan and purpose of my life.
I no longer stumble in darkness.
I now walk surely and squarely into the light.
I no longer feel the need to control my life through the ego.
I now let go and let God guide me and show me the way.
I no longer make decisions based upon egoic desires.
I now let my higher Self decide what is highest wisdom.
In every circumstance and situation,
I now allow the highest, best choice for all concerned.
I AM a walking, talking living, breathing emissary of God.
I AM God's ambassador, God's messenger.
My life is on track and on purpose.
I AM blessed and filled with the grace of God.
Thank you, God, and SO IT IS.

195. Accepting My True Purpose

Whatever prevents you from discovering, expressing, and fulfilling your true divine plan and purpose can be eliminated when you let it go.

God within me now frees and releases
All that is no longer part of the divine plan for my life.
Everything and everyone that no longer serves
The divine plan for my life now frees and releases me.
I fully accept this new divine inner freedom now.
Through the power of God within me
I now recognize, accept, and follow the divine plan of my life,
As it is revealed to me, step by step.

I rejoice in the divine plan, which is the sublime plan,
Which includes health, wealth, happiness,
And perfect self-expression for me, now and always.
I know God in me now reveals, unfolds, and manifests
The divine plan of my life now, quickly and in peace,
With perfect divine order and timing,
Under God's grace, in God's own wise and perfect ways.
Thank you, God, and SO IT IS.

196. Achieving Success

When you affirm success in your life, you achieve it, naturally.

Success comes quickly, powerfully, and irresistibly
In every phase and aspect of my life now.
The spirit of success is now working in and through me,
I AM in all ways guided, prospered, and blessed.
I AM ardent, motivated, zealous, and irrepressible.
I AM successful in all my endeavors, for the good of all.
I AM an achiever, attracting good.
I AM a winner. I AM always victorious.
I AM positive, optimistic, self-assured, and faith-filled.
Each day brings new achievements.
The mark of success is upon me.
Thank you, God, and SO IT IS.

197. Faith and Trust in God

In order to be successful, you must have faith. Worry, doubt, fear, and anxiety disappear when you put trust in God. All your needs are met, when you know God sustains you.

I have the kind of confidence
That is founded on my faith in God.
I AM faith in action, faith in activity.
I AM faith eternally sustained.
I breathe in life fully.
I relax and trust the flow and process of life.
God is preparing my way
As divine order is restored and hope is renewed.
God places divine desires in my heart
And causes them to manifest.
I take no thought of things of the morrow,

But seek first the kingdom of God today,
Knowing that all good shall be added unto me.
Thank you, God, that all my needs are met.
These words, which I now speak in faith,
Activate a law of universal good, and I accept the results.
Thank you, God, and SO IT IS.

198. Miracles Working in My Life

God can and does work miracles in your life when you ask with faith and know with conviction that your good comes to you.

With God all things are possible.
All things whatsoever I pray for,
I receive them, I accept them, and I achieve them.
As I ask, it is given to me. As I seek, I find.
As I knock, doors open for me.
Of myself I can do nothing,
But God within me can and is performing miracles
In my mind, body, relationships, finances,
And all of my affairs, right here and now.
God always makes a way where there is no way.
I have faith that God is working miracles in my life right now.
Every precious moment is a miracle.
Thank you, God, and SO IT IS.

199. Shaping and Manifesting Substance

The secret to manifestation is to tap into divine substance, from which all things in the universe are made. Learn more about this in my book *Miracle Prayer.*

God's divine substance is the source of everything.
That divine substance is available to all.
Substance is the presence of God. It does not fail.
My mighty "I AM" is the one that can shape substance.
Substance is adaptable to all my needs and demands.
The form that is necessary to my well-being now appears.
I now manifest my perfect good,
According to my true heart's desires and divine purpose.
Thank you, God, and SO IT IS.

200. Developing Perseverance

If you want to be successful, you must develop perseverance. It is not enough to make a wish. With constant focus, persistence, determination, and action, you can achieve any goal.

I AM fully merged with God's eternal presence,
Which is without beginning or end.
I AM one with God's ever-present, ever-vigilant dedication,
Which is ceaseless, perpetual, and everlasting.
I now know that I persist, persevere, and follow through
With all plans and missions that are worthwhile.
I no longer quit before reaching valuable goals.
I AM focused, determined, and intent, as God is.
I now open my heart to receive divine concentration,
Which helps me finish what I start.
I know that each day, I make progress toward my goal.
Therefore I AM enduring, patient, and calm,
As I move forward every day, step by perfect step,
In the direction of my highest good.
Thank you, God, and SO IT IS.

201. Divine Timing and Patience

Patience is an essential quality for success. When you walk steadily along a pathway, each step takes you closer to your destination, until eventually you reach your goal.

I have all the time there is: eternity.
There is time and space for everything I need to do.
I AM patient, for I trust in God's law of divine order.
There is no rush in Spirit;
Therefore, I act only when prompted from God within.
I release the past. I release the future.
I AM here now. I now live only in the present.
God's highest good comes to me at the right time,
In the right way, and in divine order.
Every experience happens to me in proper sequence.
God is in charge.
I successfully take one step at a time in my life,
And God is ever with me.

I AM at peace.
Thank you, God, and SO IT IS.

202. Divine Order and Right Action

By calling upon divine order, you can eliminate chaos and confusion, and become more orderly, organized, efficient, and successful.

Divine order is at work in the universe and in my life.
Everything in my life is in perfect, divine order now.
Through divine, right order and divine, right action,
All things in my life are in proper perspective.
I now release all careless habits and attitudes.
There is no clutter or confusion in my mind, body, or affairs.
There is only God's divine order and right action.
Every function of my mind and body is in perfect order,
For my mind and body is God's orderly temple.
No problem is too difficult to handle,
For I AM in tune with divine order.
Divine order is moving every situation forward
To perfect right results and divine resolution.
Thank you, God, and SO IT IS.

203. Achieving Excellence

Truly successful people do their best to attain excellence in areas of their lives that are significant to them. Success means making the most of your unique talents, skills, and abilities.

I AM one with the perfection that God is.
I AM perfection everywhere now.
I AM perfection here now.
I know now that I strive for and achieve excellence
In every aspect of my life.
I know now that I set precise and clear goals.
I endeavor to achieve these goals with excellence.
I know now that I do my very best in every activity.
I expect the best from myself, and I achieve the best.
No matter what my past actions have been,
I know now that every day starts with a clean slate,
And a new chance to make the very best of that day.
Every day is pristine, pure, and perfect in every way,

And I stamp my mark of excellence upon that day.
I claim my good, very good, excellent perfection now.
Thank you, God, and SO IT IS.

204. Being of Service

No one has ever attained success without putting their heart and soul into their work, and providing the greatest possible service. Go the extra mile for everyone you meet, and you can become successful.

As God gives life to everything in the universe,
I give my full commitment to everyone around me.
I now do, every day, all that can be done that day.
I take care to do each act with service and dedication.
Unto each person I encounter, I give greater value
Than whatever I receive from him or her.
I AM inspired, motivated, aroused, and moved
To be helpful and uplifting, and to brighten the day
Of every individual I meet on my pathway.
As I AM of service, I find positive responses everywhere,
Which increases my influence and brings me great success.
Thank you, God, and SO IT IS.

205. Expressing Gratitude

Gratitude is essential to success. Therefore, give gratitude often, for every gift you receive from God.

Thank you, wonderful God.
My heart overflows with gratitude.
Thank you, God, that you walk with me always.
Thank you, God, that I now receive
Your perfect blessings and grace.
Thank you for today and every day.
Thank you for your perfect presence
In, through, and as me, as all creation.
Thank you, God for this precious moment,
And for every precious moment.
Thank you, God, that I AM one with you,
Now and always.
Thank you, God, and SO IT IS.

206. Becoming Influential

There is nothing more influential than God. Therefore, to become be influential, attune yourself to the presence and power of God. Make every moment count.

I AM unified with the divine radiance that God is.
My life is filled with light. I radiate light to everyone.
I AM a light beacon, and my light shines to everyone, everywhere.
My positive energy and smooth, calm, unbristled emotional state
Radiate optimistic vibrations to everyone around me.
I AM a positivity magnet. All that is positive sticks to me.
My life is an inspiration and a lighthouse.
I do not follow the road of others. I make my own pathway.
Those who need support are encouraged by me,
As I joyously show them the way.
Thank you, God, and SO IT IS.

207. Developing a Winning Personality

Nothing in the universe is more enchanting, charismatic, and fascinating than God. Every bit of charm and personality you express is a reflection of the sunshine of God's love.

I AM one with the sunshine of God's love.
I AM the love that God is—radiant, brilliant, and shining.
I AM interesting, because I AM interested.
I AM fascinating to other people,
Because I AM fascinated by other people.
I no longer put my ego's needs ahead of others'.
I now put others' needs ahead of my ego.
I now know my care for others
Is greater than my own egoic needs.
I now know my service to others
Is more important than service to my ego.
I have a winning personality now.
Thank you, God, and SO IT IS.

208. Attaining Recognition and Prominence

When you hide your light, for fear of being criticized, you are not doing justice to who you really are. By expressing yourself and attaining prominence, you bestow honor and respect on God, as you express your talents as a gift of grace.

I AM the light that God is.
My light shines and radiates to all around me.
I no longer hide the light that I AM.
I now express who I AM without fear.
I no longer suppress my talents and abilities.
I now develop and nurture my gifts and aptitudes.
I no longer try to blend in, be "normal," or be like others.
I now let myself be my own Self.
For I AM unique and original. There is no one else like me.
I allow myself to be exactly as God made me to be:
Genuine, natural, open, and free, as my Self and me.
I AM loved, because I AM loving to others.
I AM cherished, because I cherish others.
I AM a celebrity, because I celebrate others.
Thank you, God, and SO IT IS.

209. Treatment for Perfect Divine Order and Timing

This is a treatment for myself, [*full name*], for perfect divine order and timing in every phase and aspect of my life, or better, now.

I recognize there is one divine lawgiver in the universe: God the good, omnipotent. God is the great organizing principle and power, the perfect designer of true patterns, the perfect unfoldment of all true expression and action, now. God is the source of stability and order. God is the one perfection at work in the cosmos. God works through the power of divine order.

I AM one with God's absolute order and perfection now. I AM one with the law of divine order and the law of right action. God's highest good comes to me at the perfect right time, in the right way, and in divine order. The orderly divine rule of the universe orders my life now. God's law of divine order is now established in my mind, body and affairs. Divine order is at work in my life now, and I AM harmoniously tuned to this law of divine order in every phase and aspect of my being. The inflow and outflow of everything in my life is established in divine order and harmony.

I therefore claim for myself, [*full name*], perfect divine order and timing in every phase and aspect of my life, or better, now.

I accept, in consciousness, perfect divine order and timing now. I now heal and release all thoughts that interfere with this claim, whether known or unknown, conscious or subconscious. My thoughts are now one with, the same as, and in tune with God's thought. I discharge from my mind any chaotic or unclear thinking. I release all disorder, chaos, unworthiness, disarray, discord, confusion, lack, incoherence, and inconsistency now. These thoughts are now released into God's sphere of Perfection Everywhere Now. I now welcome and embrace thoughts of divine order, divine timing, divine perfection, precision, logic, intelligence, clarity, wisdom, strength, harmony, and coherence now.

I AM in control. I AM the only authority in my life. I AM divinely protected by the light of my being. I close off my aura and body of light to all but my own God Self. Divine order is the law of my mind, body, and affairs. I AM always in the right place, doing the right thing at the right time. My every desire has its perfect right time and place for fulfillment. I trust in God and in my Self now. All is well in my life now. My life is in perfect divine order and timing now.

I now fully accept, in consciousness, perfect divine order and timing in my life now. I thank God for divine order and timing now. I release this treatment into the perfect order of God's divine law now, knowing it demonstrates now, under grace, in perfect order. Thank you, God, and SO IT IS.

210. Treatment for Optimizing Opportunities

This is a treatment for myself, [*full name*], for the perfect optimization of all favorable circumstances and opportunities, or better, in my life now.

I now recognize there is one power and one presence at work in the universe and in my life: God, the good, omnipotent, and omniscient. God is the source of everything in the universe, the creator of all life and the giver of all boons. God is the generator of all opportunity, synchronicity, serendipity, good luck, and good fortune. God is perfection everywhere now. God is perfection here now.

I AM now one with, merged with, aligned with, and the same as God. In God, I live, breathe, move, and have my being. I AM the one power and presence, the source of all good. I AM oneness and wholeness. Within me lies the source of all boons, all opportunity, synchronicity, serendipity, good luck, and good fortune. I AM perfection everywhere now. I AM perfection here now.

I now therefore know and claim for myself, [*full name*], the perfect optimization of all favorable circumstances and opportunities, or better, in my life now.

I now release from my mind any and all thoughts, feelings, emotions, and beliefs that no longer serve me, whether known or unknown, conscious or unconscious. My mind is now one with, filled with, and attuned to God's mind. I now release from my mind any and all thoughts of hesitation, missed opportunities, procrastination, pessimism, laziness, self-destruction, self-sabotage, fear of the unknown, apathy, worry, doubt, mistrust, limitation, rejection, failure, disharmony, and misfortune. And they are now gone. They are burned in the fire of God's love.

I AM now permeated with powerful, positive, beautiful thoughts and emotions of certainty, decisiveness, willingness, action, drive, ambition, energy, performance, excellence, determination, motivation, achievement, accomplishment, success, optimism, self-empowerment, self-worth, self-love, self-esteem, life, courage, trust, faith, calm, centeredness, limitlessness, acceptance, opportunity, harmony, synchronicity, serendipity, and good fortune. I welcome all these thoughts now. And they are mine.

I AM in control. I AM the only authority in my life. I AM divinely protected by the light of my being. I close off my aura and body of light to all bad luck, and I now welcome good luck into my energy field, now and always. I now know whenever any opportunity arises, I make full use of it, now and always. I claim my good, very good perfection, now and always.

I now fully accept, in consciousness, the perfect optimization of all favorable circumstances and opportunities, or better, in my life now. I thank God for manifesting this good and this good luck in my life now, under God's grace and blessings, in God's own wise and perfect ways. Thank you, wonderful God, and SO IT IS.

Enjoying Happiness

Most people are about as happy as they make up their minds to be.
—Abraham Lincoln

Everyone seeks greater happiness. Yet few can claim they are truly happy. Does happiness arise by attaining a certain status, or by finding the love of your life? All the great masters and religious scriptures tell us happiness can only be found within. Nothing outside of your Self can bring genuine lasting happiness.

If you chase happiness in the things of this world, you will eventually become disillusioned. No matter how much stuff you acquire, how much you are admired or loved, how much money, status, or prestige you get, how famous you are, how many accolades you receive, how many children you raise, how much you travel, how thin and beautiful you are, how expensive your house, car, designer clothing, and diamond jewelry, you will never find lasting happiness from any of these.

The only real happiness comes from inner contentment, acquired from living a genuine, purposeful, and meaningful life, for the good of all. When you connect with who you really are, and express your true talents and abilities, in service to others, then you realize true, lasting contentment.

211. Being Happy

Happiness comes from within, where the presence of God is the wellspring of comfort, joy, and contentment. By unifying with God, you can attain peace.

I now know, at the center of my being,
Here lies happiness, joy, content, and fulfillment.
Whatever sadness and pain I have endured
Is now lifted into the light of God's perfect peace.
I AM at rest in the heart of God's love.
I find comfort in the loving arms of God's presence.
I find joy within, at the center of my being.
I AM the joy that God is. I AM the fulfillment that God is.
Therefore I AM happy. I AM content. I AM at peace.
Thank you, God, and SO IT IS.

212. Fulfillment and Contentment

God is totality and oneness. Therefore there is nothing other than God. When you align yourself with God's presence, then all is fulfilled and nothing can possibly be missing or amiss.

God is complete, perfect, and whole.
There is nothing missing from God.
God is the one source of satisfaction.
God is fullness and utter contentment.
I now merge fully and completely
With the holy presence of God, in the center of my being.
Therefore, I AM complete, perfect, and whole.
I AM utterly content, and nothing is missing from me.
I now imbibe and express God's divine, loving qualities.
I now think, speak, and act as God's representative.
I do the works of God, for the good of all humankind.
I manifest God's compassion and forgiveness.
Therefore, I share God's joy with all around me.
I AM the happiness that God is. I AM the joy that God is.
I AM fulfilled. I AM content.
Thank you, God, and SO IT IS.

213. Expressing Joy

Joy is your true nature. When you realize who you really are, happiness becomes your daily experience.

I AM pure joy. I AM a bringer of joy.
I bring pleasure, happiness, and cheer to myself and others.
My sense of humor lightens and brightens myself and others.
I AM the joy of life, and I express joy now and always.
Joy flows through me with every heartbeat.
I now love my life. My channels of joy are wide open.
I AM now completely open to life's joy and happiness.
Thank you, God, and SO IT IS.

214. Song of Celebration

As you celebrate each day with gratitude, and praise every day as a day of grace and joy, your life is filled with miracles and wonders.

My soul sings a song of joy and celebration in God.
My kind and loving words

Gladden my heart and the heart of others.
I live in the ever joyous now. My life is joy.
I embrace the joy and wonder this day holds.
I rejoice in this day the Lord has made,
And in what God is fulfilling through me now.
Thank you, God, and SO IT IS.

215. Path of Inner Contentment

True contentment arises from within, when you make God your first priority and establish yourself in the presence of God's love.

I now allow God to guide me on my way.
I walk the path of God, as my heart is filled with peace.
I find contentment within, in simplicity.
I AM touched by divine inspiration.
I AM enlightened by divine illumination.
I AM strengthened by divine integrity.
I AM elevated by divine wisdom.
I AM fulfilled by divine love.
I now let go and let God into my heart and mind.
I AM happy. I AM at peace.
Thank you, God, and SO IT IS.

216. Accepting What Is

You will never feel complete unless you fully accept life as it is, right now. By fully accepting and embracing the present moment, you find true spiritual contentment.

Whatever is, is perfect,
For it can be no other way.
Whatever is, can only be perfect,
For all that is, is perfection.
I now accept what is, right now.
For what is, is all there is, right now.
I now live in the present moment,
In complete acceptance of what is, right now.
I AM complete. I AM whole.
I AM fulfilled. I AM at peace.
Thank you, God, and SO IT IS.

217. Happiness Right Now

People imagine they will be happy when "such-and-such" happens. However, when they achieve that, they are not content, but instead seek the next thing they think will make them happy. If you cannot be happy in this present moment, then you will never be happy in any moment.

Whatever I have imagined would make me happy
Is no longer required to make me happy.
For I AM already happy as I AM, right here, right now.
I now let go of all illusory cravings and addictions
That have prevented me from being happy right now.
I AM content with my life exactly as it is, right now.
I AM filled with calm satisfaction and equanimity.
I AM filled with inner peace, now and always.
Thank you, God, and SO IT IS.

218. Peace Prayer

To be at peace is to be happy and fulfilled. There is nothing more satisfying than the sublime experience of peace.

May God's love fill and surround me with love and peace.
May God's grace fill and surround me with grace and peace.
May God's joy fill and surround me with joy and peace.
May God's faith fill and surround me with faith and peace.
May God's light fill and surround me with light and peace.
May God's wisdom fill and surround me with wisdom and peace.
May God's strength fill and surround me with strength and peace.
I AM beloved. I AM at peace.
Thank you, God, and SO IT IS.

219. Peace of Mind

Inner peace is the sure way to true contentment. When your mind is at peace, then happiness follows.

Peace, peace, be still. Be still and be at peace.
Peace, peace, be still. Be still and be at peace.
God's indwelling presence blesses me with peace of mind.
Knowing God is my constant source of peace,
I AM secure and confident.
My mind is now relaxed, calm, centered, tranquil, and serene.
I AM deeply centered and peaceful in every area of life.

I AM at peace just where I AM.
As God's instrument of peace,
I live in harmony with my environment.
Thank you, God, and SO IT IS.

220. Treatment for Inner Peace

This is a treatment for myself, [*full name*], for perfect inner peace, or better, now. God is perfect peace and serenity. God's peace permeates and envelops the universe. God is wholeness, oneness, and contentment. God is at rest, even amidst turbulent seas of life. God is the river of tranquility. God is the light of life, the fountainhead of harmony. God is the arbor of quietude and infinite stillness. God is the constant source of peace.

I AM one with God's peace now. I AM peace. I AM stillness, quietude, and tranquility now. I AM at rest and at peace in the midst of all activity now. Knowing God is my constant source of peace, I AM serene and confident. I AM an instrument of God's perfect peace in my world now.

I therefore claim for myself, [*full name*], perfect inner peace, or better, now.

I now heal and release all limiting concepts interfering with this claim, whether known or unknown, conscious or subconscious. My thoughts are now one with, the same as, and in tune with God's thought. I renounce and release all anxiety, worry, fear, turbulence, and confusion from my mind now. These negations are dissolved by God's light, and they flow into the ocean of God's peace. I dissolve all thoughts of straining to accomplish, all feelings of compulsion or obsession, and all tension from my mind and body now.

I allow my mind and body to settle down to a state of perfect peace. I allow God to fill my mind and heart with quietude as I open myself to God's healing love. God's peace is at work in my life now, bringing me tranquility and stillness. I AM confident, stable, and my stability comes from within. I let go and let God do perfect, peaceful work through me now. I relax and turn over the results of my actions to God. I trust in God now. I AM in harmony and peace.

I now fully accept, in consciousness, my perfect inner peace, or better, now. I thank God for bringing inner peace now. Thank you, God, and SO IT IS.

221. Treatment for Inner Happiness

This is a treatment for myself, [*full name*], for perfect inner happiness, or better, now. I now recognize God is divine joy. God is the peaceful garden of happiness and fulfillment. God is the one source of satisfaction in the universe. God is perfect oneness and divine bliss. God is the endless wellspring of pleasure and delight. God is fullness and utter contentment. God is wholeness and oneness. Nothing is missing from the completion that God is.

I AM now one with, merged with, united with, and aligned with God, in a perfect, seamless wholeness. God and I are one—perfect, complete, and whole. I AM divine joy, happiness, and fulfillment. Within me, in the center of my being, is the source of all satisfaction, oneness, and divine bliss. I AM the endless wellspring of pleasure and delight. I AM fullness, wholeness, oneness, and utter content. Nothing is missing from me, for I AM the completion that God is.

I now therefore claim for myself, [*full name*], perfect inner happiness, or better, now.

I now release, loose, and let go of all thoughts, feelings, and emotions that have curbed and constrained my inner happiness now. Whatever dissatisfactions and cravings that have held my mind in bondage are now dissolved and let go, and they are gone. I AM now filled with satisfaction, peace, and contentment. I release from my mind all feelings of unhappiness, sadness, pain, and discontent. These feelings are burned in the fire of God's love. I AM now filled with happiness, comfort, and content. I AM filled with the joy that God is. I AM filled with the love that God is. I AM at peace.

I now accept fully, in consciousness, my perfect inner happiness, or better, now. I now thank God for manifesting this good in my life, under God's grace, in perfect ways. Thank you, wonderful God, and SO IT IS.

222. Treatment for Contentment

This is a treatment for myself, [*full name*], for perfect contentment, or better, now. I now know and recognize there is one presence and one power at work in the universe: God the good, omnipotent. God is the one source of complete, utter satisfaction and contentment. God is the ultimate fulfillment. God is the end of all seeking. God is the final destination of all roads.

I AM now merged fully and completely with God. This mighty "I AM," the higher Self within me, is the one presence and one power at work in my life. I AM good, very good, and perfect, complete, and whole. I AM the source of complete, utter satisfaction and contentment. Within me is supreme fulfillment. I AM the end of all seeking. All roads lead to my own inner being and the inner divinity within me.

I therefore now know and claim for myself, [*full name*], my perfect contentment, or better, now.

I now release from my mind any and all thoughts, beliefs, habits, and conditions that no longer serve me. I let go of all negative thoughts that have prevented and blocked my perfect contentment now. I now loose, let go, and dissolve all thoughts of anger, resentment, fear, guilt, blame, sadness, pain, unworthiness, frustration, discontent, dissatisfaction, disillusion, depression, regret, and disappointment. These error-thoughts are now lifted, healed, dissolved, and completely let go now, and they are gone.

I now welcome and accept wonderful, positive, life-supporting thoughts and emotions that lead me to my highest good. I now affirm new, beauteous, creative thoughts and emotions of forgiveness, gratitude, patience, faith, trust, confidence, responsibility, happiness, comfort, worthiness, satisfaction, fulfillment, content, inspiration, happiness, celebration, and rejoicing.

I AM in control. I AM in contentment. I AM the only authority in my life. I AM divinely protected by the light of my being. I AM a child of God, living in the heart of God's love. I AM a radiant light bearer—powerful, strong, happy, and fulfilled. Every moment of my life is a miracle, and I live in perfect gratitude. I AM content with what I AM and what I have. I AM perfect exactly as I AM, right here and now.

I now fully accept, in consciousness, my perfect contentment, or better, now. I now thank God for my perfect contentment. I now release this prayer into the Spiritual Law, which is at work on it, manifesting this claim right now, under God's grace, in wise and perfect ways. Thank you, wonderful God, and SO IT IS.

Transforming the Planet

I am only one, but I am one.
I cannot do everything, but I can do something.
And because I cannot do everything,
I will not refuse to do the something that I can do.
What I can do, I should do.
And what I should do, by the grace of God, I will do.
—Edward Everett Hale

Those who work in politics and social reform would argue that the way to effect planetary change is to wage war, or to sign laws, treaties, and other pieces of paper. Those who understand spiritual principles know there is only one way for the planet to change: people must change.

My spiritual mentor, Maharishi Mahesh Yogi, with whom I studied in residence for 22 years, often used an analogy. He said that for a forest to be green, each tree must be green. For the world to be at peace, each individual must be at peace. In fact, he conducted many experiments to prove this point. He discovered when large groups of people meditated together in war-torn areas, the conflict would settle down. When they meditated together in dangerous urban areas, the crime rate would decrease. He proposed that when a certain percentage of the world population meditated, the planet would be at peace and in ecological balance.

From the perspective of Spirit, nothing can be done to change the world unless people change. Therefore, as individuals, each person is responsible for contributing to world conflict or peace, to ecological balance or imbalance. If you think, speak, and act peacefully and responsibly, then you contribute to world peace and balanced ecosystem. If you think, speak, or act with disharmony, then you add to conflict, crime, war, and ecological disasters.

By using the prayers in this chapter, and by acting responsibly in harmony with our planet, you can do your part to make this world a better place.

223. Declaration of Peace on Earth

Nations and people have declared war on each other ever since people have existed. It is time for us to now declare peace!

We now declare peace on all countries.
We now declare peace on all peoples.
We now declare peace on earth.
Let there be peace on earth, right here and now.

Let the world live in peace, harmony and happiness.
Let the world live in brotherly love and unity.
Thank you, God, and SO IT IS.

224. Peace Begins With Me

When enough individuals radiate peace, peace on earth will occur naturally. Peace on earth begins with your every thought, word, and deed.

I AM the center of peace. I AM the circumference of peace.
Peace radiates from within me, to all around me.
Peace vibrates outward from the center of my being.
My inner peace touches everyone, everywhere.
I AM a peace-bearer, a peace-harbinger.
The peace that radiates from the center of my being
Is contagious and infectious; it spreads everywhere.
The peace I bring to the planet starts right here,
For I AM the source of peace and harmony.
Let there be peace on earth, and let it begin with me.
Thank you, God, and SO IT IS.

225. Make Peace, Not War

Peace is a mighty power that can overcome hatred, conflict, injustice, and war. So in this prayer, we make peace, not war. We now declare "peace on war."

We now declare peace on war.
All seeming appearance of war on this planet,
Anywhere, anytime, anyplace, is now lovingly
Dissolved, healed, released, forgiven, lifted,
And let go, into the light of God's love and truth.
We declare peace on all seeming war and conflict.
We declare peace on all seeming hatred and prejudice.
We declare peace on all seeming intolerance and injustice.
We declare peace on all that does not serve
The highest good of all on the planet.
We now accept and welcome world peace.
Thank you, God, and SO IT IS.

226. Prohibition on War

Let us now visualize a world where war is outlawed, banned, and no longer allowed to exist. That would be a place of love for all people to enjoy.

We declare a planetary prohibition on war.
All war on this planet is now banned and forbidden.
All seeming appearance of war
Is now lovingly dissolved, healed, lifted, released,
And completely let go, into the light of God's love.
We are now a planet of peace.
We are now a world of wonderment.
We are now an earth of ecstasy.
Thank you, God, and SO IT IS.

227. Overcoming Crime

No laws, statutes, jails, prisons, or executions will ever prevent crime. Only when enough people are peaceful and loving, crime will then no longer exist.

We now know and affirm that the world population
Lives in harmony and prosperity.
We declare planetary utopia now,
For all live in peace and contentment.
This planet is a safe haven for all,
And crime is now banished from the earth.
There is mutual respect amongst all peoples,
For all living beings are honored, valued, and revered.
All living beings take responsibility for themselves.
Blame, guilt, shame, and victims no longer exist.
Condemnation and punishment no longer exist.
All beings now forgive and are forgiven.
Therefore, crime and criminals no longer exist.
Thank you, God, and SO IT IS.

228. Harmony With Nature

Let us attune to nature's harmony and live according to natural law. Knowing we are one with all of life, we find harming living beings to be unthinkable.

I AM in harmony with Mother Nature.
I AM in unity with all of life.
I AM one with all the four directions.
I AM one with the sky, the earth, and the water.
I AM one with the fire, the air, and the ether.

I AM one with all time and all space.
I AM one with all living things.
I AM one with the animals and the plants.
I AM one with the land and the minerals.
I AM one with all of nature.
Thank you, God, and SO IT IS.

229. Blessing Living Creatures

As we bless the beings that inhabit this planet, we dedicate ourselves with love and respect to all living things.

Whether human, animal, plant, or mineral,
All beings on this planet are children of God.
They are created and sanctified by the light of God.
All beings are now blessed and lifted
Into the comfort of God's unconditional love,
The brilliance of God's healing light,
And the grace of God's sacred presence.
God's light shines equally upon all creatures,
And God's compassion is merciful unto all beings.
Therefore all living things on this earth
Are now cherished, blessed, and graced
With divine love, respect, honor, esteem, and reverence.
Thank you, God, and SO IT IS.

230. Treatment to Restore Ecological Balance

This is a treatment for the planet to restore perfect ecological balance, or better, now.

We now know God is perfect harmony and balance. God is the creator of the universe and all living things. God is life force energy and gives life to all. God is nature and natural law. God is the state of perfect equilibrium—the generator, operator, destroyer, and regenerator of all that exists.

I AM now one with, merged with, and united with God. God and I are one. I stand at the center of perfect balance. I AM one with restoration of perfect ecological balance. I AM one with the creator of all living things: God the good, omnipotent. I AM one with the life force energy that is God, which gives life to all. I AM one with nature and with natural law. I AM perfect equilibrium. I AM one with God: the generator, operator, destroyer, and regenerator of all that exists.

I now therefore claim, for and with the planet, perfect ecological balance, or better, now.

I now know the planet is restored to perfect ecological balance. I now call upon Mother Earth to release, dissolve, and let go of all seeming imbalance in her ecosystem. Any and all unnatural, abnormal, deviant, deleterious human errors and consequences that have caused damage to the ecosystem are now lovingly forgiven, healed, blessed, dissolved, released, lifted, and let go now. They are now gone.

I now open my heart to welcome and accept new, powerful, positive thoughts of restoration and renewal. I now know the earth is returned to its pure, natural state of ecological balance. I now know the operations of the natural forces that create, maintain, destroy, and regenerate the universe and all within it are now in perfect balance, returning the planet to love and harmony. I now know the population of this earth lives in perfect accord with Mother Nature. No matter how large the human population, the earth still maintains her balance.

I now fully accept, in consciousness, the restoration of earth's perfect ecological balance, or better, now. I now release this prayer into the Spiritual Law of Perfection Everywhere Now, knowing it does demonstrate right now, under the grace and blessings of the Divine Mother, in perfect ways. Thank you, God, and SO IT IS.

231. Treatment to Save Endangered Habitats

This is a treatment for the planet to save endangered habitats, or better, now.

I now recognize God is the safe haven, the place of perfect refuge. God is the preserver of all life, the maintainer of the perfect balance of nature. God is perfect harmony and divine equanimity.

I AM now one with, merged with, and the same as God. I live, breathe, move, and have my being in the presence of God. I AM now one with God, the safe haven, the place of perfect refuge. I AM one with the preserver of all life, the maintainer of the perfect balance of nature. I AM perfect harmony and divine equanimity.

I now therefore know and claim, for and with the planet, the perfect saving of endangered habitats, or better, now.

I now see and visualize the precious ecosystems and natural habitats of the earth are now preserved in their pristine, pure, harmonious form. I now see the rainforests, wetlands, prairies, forests, oceans, mountains, and all other precious earth habitats are preserved, maintained, and nurtured. I now visualize that human encroachment upon natural habitats is receding, and I now see humans caring for the planet with compassion, as guardians of our precious Mother Earth.

I know and accept now the plants, animals, insects, humans, and all other beings on this planet live in perfect harmony. I see all the wondrous species on earth dwelling in divine synchronicity and cosmic order. I now know this is a world of love, compassion, and wisdom.

I now therefore accept, with full conviction, for and with the planet, the perfect saving of endangered habitats, or better, now. I now release this prayer into the Spiritual Law of Perfection Everywhere Now, knowing it does manifest right here and now, under God's grace, in perfect ways, with divine compassion. Thank you, God, and SO IT IS.

232. Treatment for the Food Supply

This is a treatment for the planet to preserve its natural, organic, healthy food supply, or better, now.

I now recognize God is the giver of all life and maintainer of all health. God is perfect well-being and great robust health. God creates life. God is the cornucopia of abundant, healthy, hearty, life-giving foods. God makes and nourishes the seeds, plants, animals, and all living creatures. God creates, sustains, destroys, and re-creates, according to the operation of the laws of nature, in perfect harmony.

I AM now one with God, the creator of life, giver of life, and maintainer of health. I AM one with God's perfect well-being and robust health. I AM one with the cornucopia of abundant, healthy, hearty, life-giving foods. I AM one with God, who makes and nourishes the seeds, plants, animals, and all living creatures. I now unite with God, who creates, sustains, and destroys, according to the operation of the laws of nature, in perfect harmony.

I therefore know and claim, for and with the planet, the perfect preservation of its natural, organic, healthy food supply, or better, now.

I now know the planet's food supply is now restored to perfect balance and harmony. Any and all harmful genetic modification, damaging pesticides, depletion of the soil, and any detrimental farming and livestock practices are no longer allowed to thrive on this planet. All such harmful practices are now abandoned, in favor of life-supporting, positive practices that restore and maintain balance of the earth's natural ecosystem.

I now know, for and with this planet, that the land and soil are treated with respect so its natural nutrients and health-giving benefits are maintained and enhanced. I know that heirloom and organic seeds are preserved, and the organic and heirloom industries thrive. I now know the organic livestock, milk, cheese, poultry, fish, and egg industries thrive. I know harmful genetic modification of seeds and plants is now outlawed. I now know all genetically modified foods are labeled as such. I now know that no company or corporation can take control of the world's food supply by creating genetically modified crops that produce sterile seeds, or by creating crops that infect neighboring farms by spreading sterile seeds.

I now know and accept the entire food supply of the planet now returns to organic foods, and life-damaging farming and livestock practices are now banned forever. I now accept, in consciousness, the perfect preservation of the earth's natural, organic, healthy food supply, or better, now.

I now thank God for manifesting the perfect, healthy food supply of the earth now, under God's grace, in God's own wise and perfect ways. I now release this prayer into the Spiritual Law, knowing it does demonstrate right now in the life of the planet, under grace, in perfect ways. Thank you, God, and SO IT IS.

233. Treatment to Heal the Waters

This is a treatment to heal the waters of the earth, or better, now. I now know there is one power and one presence in the universe and in my life: God the good, omnipotent, omnipresent, and omniscient. I now recognize that God embodies the water. God's love fills the water. God's light shines through the water. God's wisdom preserves the water. God's energy gives life to the water. God is the divinity in water.

I AM now one with God, in perfect harmony and divine love. I AM one with the one power and presence of God, the omnipotent, omnipresent, and omniscient. I AM now one with God's love that fills the water with beauty and wisdom. I AM one with the wisdom, life energy, and divinity in water.

I now therefore know and claim that all the waters of the earth are healed, or better, now.

I now call upon the Holy Spirit, the spirit of truth, light, wholeness, and oneness, to shine its perfect light upon all waters of the earth, right here and now. I now know all contamination and poisoning of the waters ceases right now. I see the consciousness of humanity now lifts to a higher, acute awareness of the vital, urgent necessity of preserving the purity of the waters. I now see it becomes illegal, immoral, and impossible for human beings to pollute any waters of the earth, on land and on sea, now.

I now see the waters of the earth are honored and treated as sacred. All the waters of the earth are blessed, consecrated, hallowed, and revered. The waters of the earth are sanctified by the grace of God. All the waters of the earth are now raised to a higher vibration of purity, peace, love, joy, and grace. The waters of the earth are now vibrating on a higher octave—an octave of divine love and light.

I now and accept fully, in consciousness, the complete healing of all waters of the earth, or better, now. I now give gratitude to God for this healing, knowing it does demonstrate right here and now, everywhere on the planet, with God's pure blessings and grace. Thank you, God, and SO IT IS.

Creating Heaven on Earth

We look forward to the time when the Power of Love will replace the Love of Power. Then will our world know the blessings of peace.
—William Gladstone

Since I was a small child, I remember praying one prayer only—for world peace. That is why, in 1967, I was delighted to meet a great soul with the same vision—my mentor Maharishi Mahesh Yogi, founder of Transcendental Meditation, with whom I studied for 22 years. His primary mission was to bring about world peace. I believe his influence on creating world peace was greater than just about anyone else in the 20th century, because he single-handedly made *meditation* a household word in the West, as he taught millions of people to meditate.

You might wonder what meditation has to do with world peace. In fact, it has been proven that meditation changes human physiology. With greater coherence of brain waves, slower metabolism, greater skin resistance, and lower blood pressure, meditators become calm and peaceful. With increasing numbers of calm, peaceful people, the world must, by definition, become more peaceful.

As a teen in the 1960s, living in the San Francisco Bay area, I was part of the peace revolution. We were striving toward an uprising of consciousness. It was a time of great transformation, brought about by spiritual pioneers and great luminaries who traveled from the East to lift the youth who were starving for spiritual insight. Their common aspiration was to create heaven on earth, a utopia engendered by individuals of higher consciousness.

John Lennon's anthem *Imagine* epitomizes that time. His vision, and that of other great forerunners who have led us into this new earth, is not forgotten. Now it is our duty to step up and seize the torch passed on to us. It is time to lead this planet to its destiny—an earthly paradise of peace, prosperity, harmony, love, and happiness.

The prayers in this chapter can help do just that.

234. Liberty and Freedom for All

Envision a world of liberty, where all who have been seemingly oppressed now find freedom to believe, speak, and act according to their own truth—the true desires of their heart.

We now declare liberty and freedom for all.
We now see all peoples, all nations, the entire earth,
Blessed with liberty and freedom for all.
All those who have been seemingly oppressed,
Whose beliefs, religions, and political ideas
Have been censored and smothered, are now lovingly
Freed from all shackles that have held them in bondage.
All those who have been coerced, controlled, abused,
And held in chains of suppression, are now lovingly
Lifted into the light of freedom, on wings of eagles.
We now see liberty and justice for all.
The downtrodden are now freed from their oppressors.
Whether bound by bigotry of race, religion, gender, belief,
Or any other prejudice, all peoples are now lovingly
Blessed, loved, lifted, freed, let go, and raised
Into the light of God's perfect divine justice,
Liberty, independence, self-determination,
Sovereignty, autonomy, and freedom for all.
Thank you, God, and SO IT IS.

235. Justice for All

Though this world seems unjust and immoral, divine justice is at work. On the surface, justice appears to be missing. But the reality is human beings create their own mental laws and justice, according to their own beliefs.

This is a just world created by a just God.
God treats all with an equal hand.
God sees all with equal vision.
All is perfect in this world; there is no injustice.
Whatever we perceive as injustice is an illusion,
For there is only justice for one and all.
Each person is responsible for his or her own actions,
And has created his or her own reality.
We now see the truth; the truth is perfect divine justice.
All is just and right in this world of perfect divine justice.
We now affirm perfect divine justice for one and all.
Thank you, God, and SO IT IS.

236. Planetary Well-Being

The planet needs healing, and we can pray for her to be healed and restored to perfect balance and well-being.

This planet is now soothed and comforted,
By the healing balm of God's perfect love.
The planet is now held in the arms of God—
Safe, sound, sheltered, and protected,
Under the mighty, invincible refuge that is God.
All living things on this planet are now
In harmony and accord with each other and with God.
Love is everywhere present in every heart and mind.
The planet is now healed, loved, lifted, and blessed
By the restorer of perfect balance—the presence of God.
The world is at rest in the heart of God's love,
In perfect planetary health and well-being.
Thank you, God, and SO IT IS.

237. Heaven on Earth

We can create heaven on Earth. We can live in paradise right now. This planet can rise to a higher vibrational octave and express its true divine potential.

Our planet Earth is a beauteous paradise:
A flowering, fragrant garden of delight.
Our planet Earth is an ever-flowing stream of bounty:
A cornucopia of abundant fruits, seeds, and plants.
Our planet Earth is a harmonious symphony:
A melody of purest sweetness and love.
Our planet Earth is a place of comfort and solace:
A safe haven, sheltered under the wing of the almighty.
Our planet Earth is the abode of all living things:
Nurtured and protected by the all-seeing eye of God.
Our planet Earth is a place of perfect peace:
The Elysian Fields of heaven on earth.
Thank you, God, and SO IT IS.

238. One With All Life

The truth is we are not just bound by this body. We are connected to everything and everyone in the universe. We are one with all that is.

I AM my brother and sister on this planet.
I AM all humanity made manifest here.
I AM all males and females of all ages.
I AM all creatures of the earth and sky.
I AM all nations and all political systems.
I AM all philosophies, religions, and ideologies.
I AM all races, places, and ethnicities.
I AM all states of consciousness.
I AM all beings in all realms and dimensions.
I AM the all that is.
I AM one with all life.

239. Planetary Brotherhood and Sisterhood

We can create a world of planetary harmony, brotherhood, sisterhood, and peace for all humanity. Through prayer and meditation, this world can be transformed for the good of all.

Let us envision a world where all stand together in unity:
A world where all ethnicities shake hands in harmony,
A world where differences are set aside,
A world where politics and religion do not divide,
A world where all families live in accord,
A world where giving is its own reward,
A world where friendship and compassion prevail,
A world with respect between each male and female,
A world where parents are honored by every child,
A world where human beings are loving and mild,
A world where all living things are safe and secure,
A world free from violence, hatred, and war,
A world of peace, gratitude, and brotherly love,
A world led from within, with guidance from above.

240. Family of God

All the people of the earth united in a loving family of harmony, happiness, oneness, and wholeness—that is the place we want to live.

The Spirit of God unites the family of God around the world.
The family of humanity unites in love and harmony.
We are all merged, united, and one in the family of God.
As a family, we treat all in our family

With love, respect, and honor.
We cherish every living being on earth.
Thank you, God, and SO IT IS.

241. Treatment for World Peace

This is a treatment for and with the earth, for perfect world peace, or better, now.

I now recognize God is the ocean of peace, the eternal sea of serenity, tranquility, composure, calm, and grace. God is the safe haven of protection, the abode of sanctuary and refuge. God is the soothing, healing balm of well-being, encouragement, comfort, and solace. God is an eternal symphony of harmony, synchronicity, accord, oneness, and unity.

God is present here, there, and everywhere, in this, that, and everything. Throughout this entire earth, God is. In this very place, God is. Therefore, God's ocean of peace is right here, right now, within me. I AM fully merged with the eternal serenity, tranquility, composure, calm, and grace that God is. I AM one with God's safe haven of protection, sanctuary, and refuge. I now imbibe God's soothing, healing balm of well-being, encouragement, comfort, and solace. I now attune to God's eternal symphony of harmony, synchronicity, accord, oneness, and unity.

I now therefore know and claim, for and with the earth, perfect world peace, or better, now.

I now know that anything unlike peace in this world is now healed, lifted, released, dissolved, blessed, and let go into the light of God's eternal truth. All that has blocked or prevented peace on earth, whether conscious or unconscious, known or unknown, is now burned in the fire of God's love.

I now release from my mind, and from the mind and heart of every living being, all thoughts of intolerance, bigotry, injustice, prejudice, arrogance, domination, antagonism, conflict, tension, hatred, hostility, cruelty, brutality, aggression, mercilessness, callousness, violence, murder, crime, warfare, and battle. These thoughts are now lovingly lifted, healed, released, and let go. And they are gone.

I now welcome positive, life-supporting, peacemaking thoughts and emotions into my mind, and into the mind, heart, and soul of every living thing. I now invite and accept thoughts of tolerance, acceptance, patience, justice, modesty, humility, inner strength, guilelessness, cooperation, support, concord, ease, comfort, unity, relaxation, love, kindness, gentleness, sensitivity, friendliness, peacefulness, respect, reverence, and honor.

I AM in control. I AM the only authority in my life. I AM divinely protected by the light of my being. I AM at peace in the heart of God. I now know the world embraces change, and that change is world peace. I know the peoples of the world now let go of their petty differences, and they now perceive the unity of all humanity. The world is in accord. The world is at peace.

I now fully accept, in consciousness, for and with the earth, perfect world peace, or better, now. I now release this prayer into the mind and heart of God, knowing it does demonstrate right now, all over the world, in God's divine will and perfect order. Thank you, God, and SO BE IT.

242. Treatment for Universal Love

This is a treatment for planetary universal love, or better, now.

There is one power and one presence at work in the universe: God the good, omnipotent, omnipresent, and omniscient. God is the all-loving, all-powerful, all-embracing, all-merciful, all-compassionate presence in the universe. God is perfect unconditional love. God's love is everywhere, within everyone and everything. All that God is, is love.

I AM now one with, merged with, aligned with, and the same as God. In God I live, move, and have my being. God is within me and all around me. I AM filled with the all-loving, all-powerful, all-embracing, all-merciful, all-compassionate presence of God. I AM merged with God's perfect unconditional love. I AM one with divine love, which is everywhere, within everyone and everything. I AM the love that God is.

I now therefore claim, for and with the earth, perfect planetary universal love, or better, now.

I now know the earth is filled, surrounded, permeated, and saturated with pure divine love. This planet is now bathed and immersed in the sea of God's love. The entire world is now healed and blessed by perfect unconditional love. The earth now overflows with the grace of divine love. All that is unloved or unloving in the planet is now lovingly released, lifted, and let go. All thought-forms and beliefs on the earth that are unlike love are now lovingly transmuted and transformed by the light of God.

I call upon the Holy Spirit, the spirit of truth and oneness, to now release from the planetary mind all thoughts of hatred, resentment, anger, blame, guilt, frustration, fear, pain, cruelty, coercion, domination, and oppression. These thoughts are lovingly dissolved, lifted, healed, released, and let go. They are burned in the fire of divine love. They are dispersed, harmless and formless, into the nothingness of which they truly are.

I now welcome and invite, into the planetary mind, powerful, positive thoughts and emotions of love, peace, forgiveness, patience, peace, self-responsibility, self-accountability, trustworthiness, self-acceptance, self-esteem, peace, satisfaction, contentment, comfort, kindness, gentleness, freedom, liberty, letting go, permissiveness, open-mindedness, and non-judgment.

I now know the mind of humanity is lifted into higher awareness, greater unconditional love, and perfect peace. Universal love is increasing in the world right now. I now know and accept, for and with the earth, the perfect planetary universal love, or better, now.

I now thank God for manifesting perfect universal love in the planet now, under God's grace, with divine blessings, right here and now. I now let go of this prayer and release it into the heart of God, which now manifests it perfectly, as spoken, or better, right here and now. Thank you, God, and SO IT IS.

243. Treatment for Heaven on Earth

This is a treatment to establish heaven on earth on this planet, or better, now.

I now know and recognize there is but one life, one mind, one power, and one blessedness in the universe—that is God. There is only one presence at work in the cosmos: God the good, perfect, complete, and whole. There is nowhere that God is not, for God is everywhere present. God is life that heals all, wisdom that guides all, and love that comforts all. God is heaven. God is paradise. God is perfection everywhere now. God is perfection here now.

I now open my heart to the sacred presence of God, and I trust in God's enduring love. I AM one with the life, mind, power, and blessedness that is God. There is only one presence at work in my life: God the good, perfect, complete, and whole. God is everywhere, and therefore, God is right here within me. At my very center of being, here God is. God's life heals me, God's wisdom guides me, and God's love comforts me. For I AM unified, merged, and one with the presence of God's love, right here and now. I AM the heaven and paradise that God is. I AM perfection everywhere now. I AM perfection here now.

I now therefore know and claim, for and with this entire planet, the perfect establishment of heaven on earth, or better, now.

I now know this planet is filled with the light of God. Every inch and atom of the planet is fully immersed in the God's love, light, and perfection. I call forth Saint Germain to bring forth his violet consuming flame, which drives, spins, boils, and sweeps throughout the planet, agitating, whirling, swirling, transmuting, transforming, cleansing, and purifying this entire world, changing it into a planet of divine light and higher consciousness. This entire planet is now lifting to a higher octave—the vibration of God Consciousness.

All limiting thought-patterns around the globe that have blocked or prevented heaven on earth are now released and let go. I now call upon the Holy Spirit to eliminate, heal, release, and let go of all thought-forms, emotions, feelings, habits, and conditions that do not serve humanity. All thoughts of limitation, duality, ignorance, negativism, pessimism, conflict, superiority, inferiority, suffering, illness, death, crime, war, and all other destructive beliefs, whether known or unknown, conscious or unconscious, are now lovingly lifted, blessed, healed, released, and let go into the light of God's love.

The entire astral cloud of negative thought-forms encircling the earth is now lovingly healed and forgiven, lifted in love, unified with truth, dissolved, released, and let go. I now cut any and all psychic ties, binding karmic bonds, and negative beliefs that have tied the earth to the astral cloud with its detrimental habits and patterns. These ties are now cut, cut, cut, cut, cut, cut, cut, cut, cut, cut, cut, cut, cut, cut, loved, healed, lifted, released, and let go.

I now know, for and with the entire world, I welcome and receive powerful, positive, new, optimistic thought-forms, emotions, and feelings. The earth is now filled with beauty, truth, limitlessness, oneness, wholeness, wisdom, enlightenment, positivism, optimism, concord, harmony, equality, liberty, robust health, well-being, life force energy, personal accountability, faith, trust, and serenity.

This earth is a paradise, filled with peace, love, and happiness. All living things now live in harmony with nature and with each other. The natural balance of Mother Earth is now in perfect equilibrium. The entire planet is a heavenly sanctuary of divine blessings and perfect grace. All beings on this planet are now in tune with God's will, expressing their true talents, purpose, and mission with great passion, resolve, and determination. Therefore, the planet makes sure and swift progress in the direction of higher good, higher light, higher consciousness, and spiritual evolution.

I now fully accept, in consciousness, the perfect establishment of heaven on earth, or better, now. I now give gratitude to God for this perfect transformation of the planet now, under grace, in God's own wise and perfect ways. I now release this treatment fully and completely into the Spiritual Law of Perfection Everywhere Now, which now manifests and demonstrates this claim now under God's grace, in perfect ways. Thank you, wonderful God, and SO IT IS.

Appendix

Recommended Reading List

By Dr. Susan Shumsky
Miracle Prayer
Exploring Auras
Divine Revelation
How to Hear the Voice of God
Exploring Meditation
Ascension
Exploring Chakras

By Catherine Ponder
The Dynamic Laws of Prayer
The Dynamic Laws of Prosperity
The Prosperity Secret of the Ages
The Prospering Power of Love

By Florence Scovel Shinn
The Game of Life and How to Play It
The Power of the Spoken Word
Your Word is Your Wand
The Secret Door to Success
The Writings of Florence Scovel Shinn

By Louise Hay
Heal Your Body
You Can Heal Your Life

By Ernest Holmes
The Science of Mind
How to Use the Science of Mind

By Joseph Murphy
The Power of Your Subconscious Mind
Your Infinite Power to Be Rich
The Amazing Laws of Cosmic Mind Power

By Frederick Bailes

Hidden Power for Human Problems

By Thomas Troward

The Creative Process in the Individual

The Edinburgh and Doré Lectures on Mental Science

By Emma Curtis Hopkins

High Mysticism

Scientific Christian Mental Practice

Self Treatments Including the Radiant I AM

By Venice Bloodworth

Key to Yourself

Golden Keys to a Lifetime of Living

Index

Acknowledgments

Thanks to all who made this book possible. My gratitude goes to everyone at New Page Books, especially Michael Pye, whose enthusiasm about this book is a great inspiration. I am grateful to Adam Schwartz and Laurie Kelly-Pye, without whose expertise this project could never come to fruition.

Thank you to my New Thought teachers, who taught me about affirmation, prayer, and the power of our word, and to all my beloved inner teachers, the beautiful divine beings of light, for continued divine guidance and for creating miracles throughout this project.

I am grateful to Maharishi Mahesh Yogi, my spiritual mentor, with whom I studied for 22 years. I give gratitude to Dr. Peter Meyer, founder of Teaching of Intuitional Metaphysics, who taught me the methods of prayer used in this book. Thanks also to Rich Bell, who wrote and contributed several healing prayers here. Thank you, Prem Raja Baba, for opening my eyes to the real power of the subconscious mind and its laws and commands. I am grateful to Rian Leichter and P.J. Worley for their generosity and hospitality, and for continuing to support and promote the beautiful teachings and wisdom reflected in this book. Thanks to Terry Cole-Whittaker for her support and friendship.

Thank you to all my students, who make all my efforts worthwhile. I give thanks to all those who participate in my educational programs.

Most of all, I am grateful to Jeff and Deborah Herman. Thank you for your consistent faith, enthusiasm, support, friendship, and loyalty. Thank you for continuing to believe in me, no matter what.

About the Author

Dr. Susan Shumsky is a foremost spirituality expert, pioneer in the self-development field, highly acclaimed and greatly respected professional speaker, New Thought minister, and Doctor of Divinity. She has authored *Divine Revelation,* in continuous print with Simon & Schuster since 1996, as well as her four award-winning books: *Miracle Prayer*, published by Random House, *Exploring Chakras, How to Hear the Voice of God*, and *Ascension*; plus the books *Exploring Meditation* and *Exploring Auras.* Her books have been published in several languages worldwide.

Dr. Shumsky has practiced self-development disciplines since 1967. For 22 of those years she lived in the Himalayas, the Swiss Alps, and other secluded areas, under the personal guidance of enlightened master from India, Maharishi Mahesh Yogi, founder of Transcendental Meditation and guru of the Beatles and Deepak Chopra. She was on Maharishi's personal staff for seven of those years. She then studied New Thought and metaphysics for another 24 years and became a Doctor of Divinity.

Dr. Shumsky has taught yoga, meditation, prayer, and intuition to thousands of students all over the world since 1970 as a true New Thought pioneer. She has been featured in *Woman's World, GQ, Cosmopolitan, Los Angeles Times, Fox News,* nationally syndicated network TV, *Weird or What?* with William Shatner, and *Coast to Coast AM* with George Noory.

She is founder of Divine Revelation, a complete technology for contacting the divine presence and listening to the inner divine voice. She now travels extensively, facilitating workshops, seminars, spiritual retreats, cruise seminars-at-sea as well as tours to India, Peru, and other sacred destinations worldwide. Dr. Shumsky also offers spiritual coaching, prayer therapy sessions, and breakthrough sessions.

On her website, *www.divinerevelation.org*, you can:

- Join the mailing list.
- See Dr. Shumsky's itinerary.
- Read the first chapter of all of Dr. Shumsky's books.
- Listen to dozens of free interviews and teleseminars with Dr. Shumsky.

- Invite Dr. Shumsky to speak to your group or teach a class in your area.
- Find Divine Revelation teachers in your area.
- See the Divine Revelation curriculum.
- Register for Divine Revelation retreats and Teacher Training Courses.
- Order CDs, DVDs, downloadable files, or laminated cards of healing prayers.
- Order books, audio and video products, or home study courses.
- Order beautiful, full-color prints of Dr. Shumsky's illustrations.
- Register for telephone sessions and teleseminars with Dr. Shumsky.
- Register for spiritual tours to sacred destinations worldwide.

When you join the mailing list at *www.divinerevelation.org*, you will receive a free, downloadable guided mini-meditation, plus access to a free weekly teleconference prayer circle and a free online community group forum.

As a gift for reading this book, please use the following special discount code when you register for one of the retreats or tours at *www.divinetravels.com*: HEALING108.

Dr. Shumsky wants to hear from you. Please share your personal experiences of instant healing by e-mailing your testimonials to divinerev@aol.com.

43 P
44